Writing for Video

Writing
for
Video

Gene Bjerke

Petrel Publishing

Williamsburg, Virginia

11-97

Publisher's Cataloging in Publication

(Prepared by Quality Books Inc.)

Bjerke, Gene A.
    Writing for video / Gene Bjerke
    p. cm.
    Includes bibliographical references and index.
    LCCN: 96-92002
    ISBN 0-9631505-3-7

    1. Videorecording—Authorship.   2. Industrial
television—Authorship   I. Title.

PN1992.7.B54 1996   808'.066791
                                            QBI96-20259

Contents

Contents

Contents

Contents

1
What is a Script?

Before we get started, it would be useful to make sure we know what it is we are talking about. Put in its simplest terms, *a video script is a blueprint for a video.* Let's go back one more step and ask, "what is a video?" (or a film) is a presentation that consists of moving pictures and a variety of sound elements presented together to achieve a certain purpose. That purpose may be to entertain, to motivate, to inform, to sell, to educate, or any combination of these. It differs from a live presentation in being recorded. It differs from a recorded lecture in that it includes visuals. It differs from a slide/sound show in that the visuals move. It differs from a computer-controlled program by not providing the element of interactiveness.

A video presentation communicates to the audience through the two most important senses that we use to understand the world around us. By far the majority of the information that comes to our brains comes through the channels of sight and sound. Sight is generally considered the more important of the two, but most of us could not even imagine what our world would be like if we were deprived of either of these faculties. These are precisely the

two channels that are employed by film and video. As a
script writer, it is up to you to make the best use of both
of these channels. But the script writer does not make the video. The
script is but a blueprint. That means that while it is the
final product for the writer, it is not the final product for
the person the script is written for, the individual member
of the audience. That person will probably never see the
script. The only people who will see the script are the
client (and anyone that person shows it to) and the
production crew. The script is written *for* the audience, but
to the production crew. Each member of the crew will start
with your script, then add something from his or her own
area of expertise to the final product. The camera person
will pick the exact angle, light, and compose each shot.
The sound person(s) will record the various kinds of sound
that may be needed: dialogue, narration, sound effects,
music, or whatever. The editor will select the shots,
combine, juxtapose, and pace them, and connect them with
the various sound elements. The director will oversee all of
this, work with any actors involved, and probably have
some input in all of the areas. The producer makes it all
happen; he or she finds the money, makes the
arrangements, and sees to it that everything gets done. In
addition, re-recording engineers, colorists, on-line editors,
any number of other people will have a hand in the creation
of the final product, though most of them will never see
your script.

As a script writer, you need to be aware of all these
people. In fact, you may *be* one or some of these people.
For purposes of this book, I am going to assume that you
are not. But the reason for bringing all of this up is that

you need to take the whole process into account. Your blueprint, your script, needs to be clear and specific so that the production crew knows what you want; but at the same time needs to give them the space to make their own contributions (they are going to take it whether you give it to them or not).

So what, exactly, is the script writer's contribution to this whole process? What does the script writer do that the others need in order to do their part? As a script writer you have two tasks: to *organize the information* and to *design the production*.

During the research phase, you will need to gather all the information you can. This will usually come to you in a rather chaotic manner. Not all the connections will be clear. If your client assures you that they have everything you need, all organized and ready to go, don't believe them. If they say they have a presentation already on slides and all you need to do is make them into a video, be aware that there is a big difference between a slide show and a video. Some of the most difficult and time-consuming research I have had to do were for clients that told me they had everything I needed. Everyone organizes information differently, so only you can organize the material for your use.

Once you have the information gathered and organized, your other big job is to design the production. You decide on which elements of the information you are going to present. You determine in what order to present them. You figure out what visuals and sound will do the job best. You choose the manner of presentation. And then you communicate all this to the production crew. All this time you must think like a director, a camera operator, a sound person, and an editor. And that is the most important skill, thinking. *All writing is thinking.* You need to have a lot figured out in your mind before you ever put fingers to keyboard.

This makes it sound as if writing a script is a difficult, complicated process. It is if you try to do everything all at once. But by breaking the process down into specific steps and procedures, you can tackle the problems one at a time and solve them.

Situations vary widely in the world of video production. Your situation may be anything from a "one-man-band" to being one cog in a giant corporate machine to working for a small production company. You may be a video production person or a corporate writer whose boss has just assigned you a video to write. Perhaps you have no writing or production experience but have something you want to express in the form of a video. Whatever your situation, the process is still the same. For purposes of this book, I am going to assume that you are a writer working alone; you have a client—the person who wants the video made; and that it will be produced by a third party—a production unit of which you are not a member. (Even if you plan to produce it yourself, you should write it as if someone else were going to produce it. Don't tell yourself "I'll remember that." You won't.)

With this situation in mind, let's put on our business clothes and go meet the client.

2
First Things First

The first meeting with the client is more than a get-acquainted session. It is true that if you have not worked with this person before, you will both be sizing each other up. You will be trying to find out what this person wants and expects (or whether they even know what they want) and the client will be making some judgements about whether you will be able to handle the job. To instill confidence, you need to look and act professional. One of the best ways is to get right down to the business at hand.

The business at hand for you at this meeting is not to find out about the subject, but to find out about the videotape itself. Don't be surprised if the client wants to launch right in to talking about the subject. However, this will do you little good until you know about the tape. So as soon as possible, swing the conversation around to the four P's of the videotape: People, Purpose, Presentation, and Production.

It may be helpful to have a sheet or two of paper set up like a questionnaire form (for an example, see Appendix A). Remember to leave lots of space for the answers. Another way to do it if you use a notebook computer to take notes is to have a template already set up that you just need to fill in. That has the advantage of being infinitely expandable. However you do it, preprinted form, computer, or yellow pad, get the information down. You will need it later, and it will be more useful to have the precise wording. You can determine this information in any order. But here, in roughly the order of importance, is what you need to know:

People

It is important to know who your audience is going to be. For example, you would not explain something to your child's fourth-grade class in the same way as to a group of engineers. There is no such thing as a generic audience. Every audience has some distinguishing characteristics. Audiences for informational tapes are often very specific.

You need to know some basic demographic information. Such things as age spread, sex ratios, education. Is this show aimed at employees? if so, at what level in the hierarchy? Is it aimed at customers? potential customers? investors?

You need to know the audience's background in the subject— what they know already, and what they think they know. Are they experts being told about a new technique or discovery? Are you giving basic information to people who know nothing at all about the subject? Or perhaps they may fall somewhere in between. They may think they know a bit, but in fact the supposed knowledge is partly or completely wrong.

Who (or what kind of person) would be the best person to deliver your message? Who do they trust or like? You need to know their likely attitude toward the subject. What do they like about the subject? What do they dislike? Are they interested, indifferent, or hostile? You especially need to know about any obstacles that must be overcome: prejudices, false ideas, sore points. These are the areas you will need to treat carefully to avoid turning the audience off.

You should learn enough to be able to visualize the members of the audience. It is often helpful if you can visualize one typical audience member and aim your presentation at that person.

Purpose

The other major body of information you need to know before you launch into the research and writing is the purpose of the tape. What, exactly, is this tape expected to accomplish? The tape may be viewed as a solution to a problem; it may be expected to inform, to teach, to sell, or to motivate. Each of these purposes will require a different approach.

Another way to look at this is that every tape is a sales tape. You might be selling goods, or you might be selling information, attitudes, enthusiasm, acceptance, or motivation. Whatever it is, you are trying hard to bring the audience to your point of view.

That is the general purpose. But you need to know the specific purpose. Exactly what are you trying to convince your audience of? You must also keep in mind that an audience can only absorb so much at one sitting. It is best if you have one major purpose. You may also include some less important points that would be nice for them to remember. One way of focussing on the major purpose is to ask, "When the tape is over, what one thing do you want to make sure everyone goes away with?" Anything in addition is extra.

This is not to say that people can only be expected to remember one thing from a videotape. But the number of points that you can reliably expect to make in one show is small. I have heard the figure of seven as the maximum number of things that can be remembered from one presentation, but I think that is high. If you can narrow the focus down to one or two major points and perhaps four minor points the tape will be most effective. If your client has a whole list of points to get across, it will be more effective to create several shorter, well-focused tapes than to make one long, rambling presentation.

When discussing purposes, concentrate on outcomes. What do you want the audience to carry away? When it is all finished, what do you want them to think, feel, or do? Another approach is to find out what changes are desired. Should the audience change an attitude? a behavior? a technique? Whatever the purpose of the show, get it stated precisely and write it down.

Presentation

You also need to get some technical information up front. One area is that of presentation. How will the audience view this tape? Will they see it one at a time or in a group? Will you have a captive audience or just people passing by (such as in a booth at a trade show)? Will there be a presenter— someone to prepare the audience, introduce the tape, and answer questions afterward? Or will it need to stand alone? Will there be supplementary materials—handouts or workbooks? If it is being shown to employees, will it be on company time? Is this part of a series? Will there be a test afterward?

Just as you need to visualize your audience, you need to put yourself in the place of the audience so that you can write a show that is appropriate to its viewing conditions.

Production

In order to write something that can be easily produced, you need to know some basic facts about the production situation. You may already be familiar with the crew and its capabilities. If so, good; if not, you need to learn the answers to certain questions.

Whether the crew will shoot on one-inch or three-quarter, component or composite, digital or analog, may be interesting but is not generally of much concern to the writer. It would be useful to know if they can handle such special techniques as Steadicam or shooting from a helicopter, though that is usually a question that comes up later in the process.

What is important to you is the question of how sophisticated their editing facilities are. It would be pointless to write a script that depends on digital effects if the production crew is limited to cuts-only editing. You do not need to know the make and model of all their editing equipment, but capabilities can be broken down into three broad categories:

The lowest level is "cuts-only." Some systems may be able to produce a fade in and a fade out, but you can't count on dissolves or wipes to ease the story along. Obviously, fancy digital effects are out of the question. What this means to you as the writer is that transitions will need to be worked out with greater care. This system may or may not include a character generator to create superimposed text.

The mid-level (and probably the most common) adds a switcher and character generator to the simple system. The switcher gives the crew the capability to move between scenes with fades, dissolves, and wipes. It can also be used to highlight areas of the frame, create split screens, and insert video in a box on screen. The character generator (CG) can be used for titles, speaker identification, and other superimposed text. Some CGs can also create colored boxes and other effects.

The mid-level can cover a wide range of capabilities. Some producers may have equipment to create computer graphics, or a range of Digital Video Effects (DVE). You probably won't need detailed knowledge of what the crew is capable of until later on in the writing process.

At the top end are the post-production houses. These are separate organizations that specialize in putting the fanciest finishing touches on a production. Post houses buy all the latest in digital equipment and can provide the producer with flips, spins, page turns, multiple images and anything else that can be imagined. They can make color corrections to the image, and even change colors within an image. You have a picture that includes two red soda cans and you want one of them green? No problem, take it to the post house. These people can perform visual magic if you have the budget for it.

And that is the other thing you need to find out. Besides getting a feel for the producer's capabilities, you need some idea of the budget for the production. You don't need the exact figure. A given number really doesn't mean much. What it will buy depends on what needs to be charged to the budget and what can be hidden elsewhere. You just need to know, in general terms, what is possible. This will tell you what kinds of things you can include in the script.

There are a number of factors that affect the cost of producing a picture. In general these are:

- ▶ Number of actors. If there is no budget for professional actors, a narrator is usually used.
- ▶ Amount of travel needed.
- ▶ Number of locations.
- ▶ Number of shooting days.
- ▶ Difficulty of shooting on any given location.
- ▶ Size of crew.
- ▶ Complicated shots, such as dolly, crane, or Steadicam shots, that take longer to shoot (crew time is expensive).
- ▶ Weather factors—a lot of exterior shots may lead to expensive down time while the crew waits out bad weather.
- ▶ Special effects (physical or optical).
- ▶ Amount and kind of music (library or composed).
- ▶ Graphics.
- ▶ Animation.
- ▶ Complex audio mixing, called "sweetening."

You probably will only get the vaguest outline of what is possible at the first meeting. As you develop the show, you may need to check back with the client or the production people on the cost of suggested scenes.

Related to production capabilities and budget is the question of schedule. There may be a shooting schedule or a release date already decided. This is information that will be helpful to you. For instance, you may have to factor in the fact that the shooting will take place in a particular season. To meet the shooting schedule, they will need the script by a certain time.

The scriptwriter normally provides three documents to the client. These are the Treatment, the First Draft Script, and the Final Script. You may be given due dates for these elements. In the situation where there is no schedule for your work, make one up for yourself. Most of us work more efficiently when we have specific goals and deadlines.

There is one other thing you need to find out. That is the approval process. In the best situation, one person will have the authority to sign off on the various stages of creating the script. The worst situation sees the script passing up the chain of command or through a committee. If this is the case, prepare yourself for a lot of time and a lot of rewrites. Try to zero in on the person with approval authority if you can. Be aware that in some cases the script may also have to be reviewed by the legal department.

Once you have all this information (it's really not as long and complicated as it may sound), you are ready to start your research. This first meeting is the time to learn where to find the information you will need. You will get your facts either from written materials or from talking to people.

The client will usually provide you with whatever written materials you need, or tell you where to find them. Another source of knowledge is the Subject Matter Expert (SME) or Technical Expert. You will often meet this person (or persons) at the initial meeting. Find out how to get in touch with them and when they will be available. You and the SME will form a team. The SME knows about the subject, you know how to use the video medium. Between the two of you, you will design the video.

Now that we know where we are going, let's get on the way. No yellow brick road for the script writer, more like hacking your way through a jungle of miscellaneous information. So let's sharpen our machetes and set off.

3
Gathering Information

Before you can write a video script, or anything else for that matter, you need to have an in-depth knowledge of the subject. If you already know your subject well—for instance, if you are a Subject Matter Expert who has been asked to write a video in your area—you are that much ahead. For the purposes of this book, we will assume that you are not. So the next step is research.

What to look for

When doing research, you will be looking for two kinds of information: *facts* and *grabbers*.

Facts are everything you need to know to understand the subject. These are the detailed pieces of information that will make up the bulk of your presentation, the What, When, Where, Why, and How of the subject.

Grabbers are facts also, but of a special kind. These are the bits of information that grab your attention. They may be facts that are unusual or unexpected, or they may be

situations that touch off emotions. These are the things that
you will use to catch and hold attention, to create interest,
and to carry your audience along. Remember, there is no
such thing as a dull subject. Someone is keenly interested
in it. Find that person, find out what excites him or her
about it. Then tune in on that excitement.

Think about butterflies for a moment. Butterflies may
not seem like an exciting subject. But when you find out
that these fragile-looking creatures migrate for thousands of
miles, that whole flocks of them arrive at the same grove
of trees on exactly the same day every year, they become
more interesting—to you and to your audience. If you can
get excited about the subject, you can excite others.

Another thing that you will be looking for is visuals.
Tape is a visual medium, so you should constantly be
asking yourself, "What can we take a picture of?" In many
cases, this is obvious. But experts who are trying to apply
basic principles to a wide range of situations will often talk
in very abstract terms. But pictures are very concrete. You
need to keep coming back to what you need with questions
like, "Can you give me an example?" and "What can we
photograph to show that?" Videotape is Show and Tell;
keep looking for what you can show.

Where to look for it

When you write a video for a client, you have a
valuable information resource—your client. In most cases,
the client has at hand all the information you will need. In
a few cases, you may have to do your own research for
part or all of the project. We will not go into research

methods here, there are whole books on that subject. I will just remind you that for library research your reference librarian is your best friend.

Another good source is experts, people who have put a great deal of study into a subject. You may find such people, or leads to such people, at your nearest college or university. Or you may go back to the library. Find out who wrote the books and articles that deal with your subject. Then contact them. And when you talk with them, ask who else is knowledgeable on the subject. The leading thinkers on any subject tend to know each other.

The information resources that your client can provide may be in the form of written material, visual material, or personnel. Let's look at the written/visual material first.

Written/visual materials

Written materials may be in the form of annual reports, research reports, technical manuals, or any other form of documentation. Visual materials may be other videotapes, films, still photographs (slides or prints), drawings, etc. These can all be treated the same as far as your research is concerned.

You will have to plow through this material. Depending on the level of detail and what you need to know, you may be able to skim some of it. The first question that comes up is, how much do I really need to know? Basically, you need to know more than will end up in the video—perhaps three times as much. You need to become a temporary expert in the subject. You usually don't know what you need to know until you already know more than you can put in the tape.

So you go through it all, looking for the facts and the grabbers that will eventually make up the content of your tape. You need to remember them all somehow. Unless you have an incredible memory, you will need to take notes. In some cases, you may just be able to pull out key pages and keep a file of them, but that is not usually the case. If you take your notes on index cards, they can be pushed around and arranged later. They are also easier to lose. You may want to take brief notes, with references to the source. However you do it, give some thought to the fact that you will have to refer back to them later.

With the exception of possible short quotes, you probably won't use written source material directly in the finished tape. The same is not necessarily true for visual materials. This means that you will be looking at these materials in a different way. First, you will look at the tapes or still pictures for the information they contain. If you think you may use the pictures, you will also have to judge their quality.

Even if you are looking at existing video strictly for its information value, it will give you some ideas about how the production crew can shoot the same or a similar subject. This is usually not a big problem. If you are thinking about using the visuals themselves as sources, they have to pass three tests. First, does the material have good visual quality? Remember that everything loses quality in the copying process. If the picture is part of a videotape that is only available as a VHS copy, it will look much worse than the original photography in the rest of the tape. You might be able to get away with using it if it is rare historical footage that can't be gotten any other way. Some-times, you can get away with using lesser-quality material

if it is in a separate sequence by itself, with definite separa-
tion from the rest of the tape. This is ultimately a decision
of the director or editor, but as a writer, you should be
aware of the possibility.

The second test is usability. The footage may look nice,
but does it really fit in with a useful approach to the
subject? In one sense, there is no such thing as stock
footage. All footage is shot from a particular point of view.
What the shooter or director wanted to say with a particular
shot determines the exact angle, lighting, etc. The shot of
the same subject that you would prefer might be different.
That said, you will often need to use footage that was shot
for a different purpose. It may be the only footage taken of
a past or remote event, or the producer may not be able to
afford to shoot that subject for this project. For these
reasons, you will from time to time need to use some
existing footage. The presence of existing footage will
affect, to a greater or lesser extent, how you treat the
material around it.

The last test is a legal one. When you use existing
visual materials, either still or motion, you are copying
someone else's work. If the client does not already own the
copyright to the work, rights will have to be bought (unless
it is in the public domain, which is unlikely). The same
applies to music—never specify a popular song for the
sound track unless your client is willing to spend a great
deal of money for it. This can become a complicated
subject. If necessary, there are people whose business it is
to get clearances for published works.

With visual material, and especially videotape sources,
you have the same problem of being able to put your hands
on it later. The easiest to deal with is stills (photos or

drawings), just put them in a separate box to hand over to the production crew. The next easiest is videotape with what is called a "window dub." Some videotapes have time code. That is a method of giving every single frame of the tape a unique number. It is in the format of *Hour:Minute:Second:Frame*. A window dub is a copy that has these numbers printed right on the picture itself, usually in a box (the "window"). You just need to include the beginning (and perhaps the end) number in your notes if you want to use a particular segment. If the tape does not have this feature, zero the counter on the VCR when you start each tape, and note the counter numbers for each section in which you are interested. This will make it easier for you or someone else to find a particular section later. But don't expect them to fine the exact same frame. No two VCRs will measure the footage exactly the same way, and in fact, the same VCR may not give a specific frame the same number twice in a row.

Subject Matter Experts

The other major resource that your client will be able to provide is access to the people who know the information. These are the Technical Experts or Subject Matter Experts (SME). You will often find yourself working with a particular SME. You and this person become a team, the SME provides the information, you put it into videotape form.

In other situations, you may not be assigned an SME. Instead you may need to talk with several people. These may be customers, members of the prospective audience, outside experts, people likely to be on camera, or anyone else that you think might provide useful input. In any case, you need to exercise interviewing skills.

Interviewing

The first rule of interviewing is to be prepared. Learn as much about the subject and your interviewee as possible before you start. While there is no such thing as a dumb question, knowing a bit of what you are after and where you want to go will give the interview focus. Figure out what you need to know and work up some basic questions beforehand. Write them down so that you don't forget one.

There is one basic rule for questions: don't ask any questions that can be answered "Yes" or "No." The object is not to have the SME, or whoever, confirm your own ideas, the object is to find out what is in the expert's mind. Phrase your questions so as to allow the interviewee scope to expand on the subject, express his or her own ideas and opinions, or even go off in another direction. The purpose of prepared questions is to make sure you get the basic information that you need, not to restrict the interplay. As the conversation goes on, you will think of follow-up questions to explore the new areas that are being uncovered. This wandering off into new territory is one of the most interesting aspects of interviewing, and can uncover useful information. Let it happen, but within limits. You don't want to get too far afield and you do want to cover the basic information. This is where the art of the interview comes in, letting the subject wander, but within a certain range.

One of the things you will need to decide is whether or not to tape the interview. There are advantages and disadvantages to using a tape recorder. Taping allows you to capture the subject's exact words. This is useful for getting direct quotes or creating believable dialogue. It also allows you to concentrate on your interviewee and not be distracted by taking notes.

On the other hand, tape recorders occasionally break down. I can recall taping an interview with my Mother about some events in her childhood. She had some interesting and insightful reminiscences. Later, I discovered that the tape had jammed and the recording was useless. Also, it is difficult and time-consuming to find a particular quote in a long tape. Transcribing a tape solves that problem but takes much longer than the interview itself, especially if there is a lot of background noise that makes it difficult to hear the subject.

To tape or not to tape will vary with each situation. When you do decide to tape a conversation, you should get the interviewee's permission. This is simply good manners. Taping a telephone conversation is a simple matter. Many answering machines are equipped to tape conversations if you wish. You can also get a simple device from an electronics store, such as Radio Shack, that allows you to plug a tape recorder into your phone line. Each state has regulations regarding the taping of phone conversations. Find out the regulations in your state and be sure to observe them.

There is one other use for a taped interview. You can use it later to check your own interviewing technique. When listening back to the interview, you can assess your performance in a more detached manner. The poorly-worded questions and the distractions become more obvious. If you find that you are talking more than the interviewee, you know you are in trouble.

Locations

Another form of information that you need to acquire involves locations, the places where the tape will actually be shot. Try to visit them if you can. It is possible to write a script by simply imagining the shooting locations (and in some cases you may have to do this), but actually being there and seeing them will result in a better script.

The first thing that happens is that it gives you a feeling for the situation. You know exactly what things look like and which elements can or need to be photographed. It allows you to visualize the scenes in your mind as you write. You can create more accurate scene descriptions if you know what is there and how it can best be photographed.

It is sometimes useful to take photographs of the location. The photographs will come in handy later when you try to remember what a location looked like. In addition, looking through the viewfinder gives you a cameraperson's view of the scene. It helps to keep you from specifying something unphotographable. Finally, the photos may also be useful to the crew later if the location is strange to them.

Actually seeing the location will probably give you ideas for shots. You will see things that you might not have thought of that will provide useful information. You will usually have someone along that knows the situation, either the SME or someone who works in the area. You can ask this person questions and get more useful information. This is information that arises out of and applies directly to the situation you see. This may well provide you with an angle (either a camera angle or an approach to the material) that you can use.

In some cases, you may be the only person to see the location before the crew arrives to shoot. In that case you end up being the location scout for the production. While it is not your job to check out such details as access or the amount of electrical power available, you will have to come to some conclusions as to the practicality of shooting in the situation. There is no point in specifying a shooting location, only to have someone later decide that it is impractical to do it and start making wholesale changes to your script to "work around the problem." However, with modern equipment (and a little ingenuity), there are very few places where it is not possible to get footage.

When doing photography, I find it very useful, when possible, to walk all around my subject. Everything looks different from different angles. You might find that the subject is more interesting when looked at from the opposite angle than the one from which you first saw it. This happens visually when the script writer visits a location. You get to see the scene and walk around in it. You get to look at it from different angles. The same thing is true when you think about your subject. Walk all around it, think of it from different points of view. You may find that there is a more interesting or more informative way to approach the subject than the obvious one, or the one that first came to mind.

When you have all the information in hand, or even as you are gathering information, you need to think about what is important. What is the central idea, the spine around which you will build your script? This is also another place to think about the show's title. It may well be a distillation of, or at least a reference to, the main point of the tape. But that gets us into the next step in the process.

4
Organizing Your Information

By now you should be sitting there looking at a pile of notes, manuals, brochures, tapes, or whatever. You are probably wondering what in the world you are going to do with all this stuff. What you are going to do with it is organize it. There are two ways to do this, physically and mentally. The two interact with each other, so let's get started with the physical organization.

You need to gather together things that are related. This may mean clipping together pieces of paper, or cutting and pasting. You may want to copy things over from scattered sources onto single sheets of paper. If you took your notes on index cards, you can just shuffle them into another order. If you are used to doing your thinking on a computer, you may even create a hyperdocument, complete with cross references. That may be very interesting and fun, but don't get carried away; this is not the final product, just a step along the way.

There is a certain amount of housekeeping that needs to be done at this stage. You want to make sure that everything is properly labelled. This is especially true of quotes, you don't want to attribute a statement to the wrong person. It's a good idea to keep everything for a given project in one place. You need to be able to put your hands on any individual piece of information quickly when you want it. You will be referring back to these notes throughout the project. Part of the purpose of the exercise is to impress the information on your mind so that you are ready for the other part, organizing it mentally.

Organization, Part 1

The best way to keep from being overwhelmed by the details of your research is to apply a top-down approach. Or you might think of it as working from the outside in. Just as the videotape's editor might start with a long shot to establish the situation, then work in with progressively closer shots until you are looking at a tiny detail, you should look at the long view first. Start with the large, overarching ideas and fill in the details later. It is the same process as outlining a written piece. You rough in the major headings first (the Roman numerals), then you add the major points under each (the capital letters), and then go on to the points under these (Arabic numerals, etc.).

You may want to start out by writing down what this show is about in one, brief sentence. A good place to start is with your statement of Purpose: "This tape describes and explains the new employee benefit program," for example. Then go on to the next level of detail—a list of the programs, to continue the example. Then under each of these, the details of each program. Not every subject will fall into place that neatly, but the general approach should work with just about any body of information.

This top-down approach also applies to the documents you give to your client. These are usually three in number, a treatment, a first draft script, and a final draft script. The treatment is a brief description of your vision of the film. It is very light on detail and usually only a couple of pages long. In it you say how you plan to approach the subject and give a brief, general description of what the audience will see and hear. This gives the client an opportunity to react to the general design of the show. The client will either agree and give you the go-ahead to proceed, or state specific objections for you to work around.

Once your basic approach has been approved, you will write the first (or rough) draft script. At this stage, you add more detail to the basic outline. You specify shots and write out exact dialogue or narration. This is presented in one of the script formats (more on them later). Now the client reacts to the details: are those the correct shots? Is that precisely what we want to say? Are all the details accurate?

The client will usually mark up the script with comments and corrections. You then take these detailed comments and corrections and produce the final draft script. This is the finished document that will be the blueprint for the producer.

Once you have the material organized for your understanding, you need to organize it for presentation.

Organization, Part 2

The first thing you need to decide is exactly what needs to be presented and in what order. To this end, you will approach the material you have gathered with several questions in mind. The first might well be, what information is appropriate for this audience? You neither want to bore them with what they already know, nor confuse them with a lot of facts that do not really apply to their situation. If your audience is forklift drivers in the warehouse, they will probably have no use for information that is of vital concern to middle management. Knowing what is relevant is part of knowing your audience. You can expect them to be most interested in matters that are of direct concern to them.

This leads us to a question that *you* need to ask before the audience does, namely "What's in it for me?" In a sense, every show is a sales show, and you sell something by showing that it is of value to the buyer (in this case, the viewer). Remembering that your viewer will only take away a limited amount of new information, you need to hone your presentation down to the things that are most relevant to the target audience. Stultifying detail or material that needs to be studied (for instance, all the possible options in a complicated benefits program) may best be left to a printed handout that the viewer can study at leisure, or when the need arises. The tape may only need to make the viewer aware that such a document exists, and how to use it.

Having pared the information down to the elements that you are going to present, you need to determine where to start and in what order to present them. There is a basic principle in education that you start from where the pupils are and move them to where you want them to be. This is why you need to have determined what the audience already knows about the subject. That is where they are, and that is where you start. Ideally, your first new fact or argument should have a good hook into what the audience already knows; your second hooks into the first, and so on. This will not always be possible, but it is a good model to keep in mind.

So at this point you will start from where the audience already is and proceed in a careful, stepwise manner to where you want them to end. Each step will be a smooth, logical transition from what went before.

Write each of the steps down. You may want to rearrange some of them after you have thought about it a bit, so you might want to write them on index cards, or type them into the computer. Whether you write them on cards, a computer, or a yellow pad, leave room on the right because you will be adding something to them.

This is the beginning of your "Two-Column Organizer." In subsequent chapters I will tell you how to complete it.

5
Information to Video

Once you have all your points lined up neatly, you need to turn this information into video. That is, you need to convert ideas into pictures.

Before we get into the details, let's make sure we continue to keep the overall principles in mind. People and Purpose must be kept uppermost at all times. Keep on target, don't allow yourself to be tempted down an irrelevant side path because it looks like fun.

Video is a medium that can bypass the intellect and go straight to the emotions. Keep attitudes and feelings in mind as you think about the show. What is the audience's probable attitude at the beginning? What attitude do you want at the end? What do you want them to feel? How can you make emotion work for you?

And the most important: the presentation should proceed from the material. The famous architect Louis Sullivan insisted that "Form Follows Function." Or to put it in video terms, "The Content Drives the Form." Everything you put in the tape must be there for a reason, and that reason better have something to do with the message. Given a big enough budget or a creative enough on-line editor, you can get almost any flashy effect you want. But effects for the sake of effects are counterproductive. There are several famous commercials that were full of visual fun and games. People could recall the pictures but not the product. Don't let this happen to your informational video. This doesn't mean it has to be dull; the trick is to make it interesting *and* informative. It happens when the pictures are driven by the message. That is real creativity.

Forms

There are a number of different ways that you can present any subject. You need to choose, for each part of your project, the way that works best for your audience and purpose. Here, in no particular order, are the most common:

Talking Head

Talking head generally refers to a close-up of someone looking into the camera and telling you what they want you to know. It is generally regarded as a Bad Thing, but that is probably due to its over-use. Used judiciously, it can be effective. The advantage of the talking head is its immediacy. It can have the flavor of a conversation. It is a good way to bring home a special point. Someone looks you straight in the eye and tells you something they want to be sure you understand. However, it is a bad vehicle for presenting large amounts of information. Since there is nothing to look at except this person talking, the visual quickly gets boring.

An easy trap for people to fall into is to record an interesting speaker. A person may be dynamic and spellbinding in a personal presentation. Merely videotaping this person's presentation will invariably produce a dull tape. Something vital is lost in the translation. You are not using the capabilities of the medium, and the electricity that is there in person never seems to come through.

Variations on the talking head are *demonstrations* and the use of *props*. The typical cooking show on television is an example of demonstration. This can be interesting if you concentrate on what is being demonstrated and only use shots of the presenter when they can be most effective.

Talking heads with props are usually not very interesting, but there have been some notable exceptions. For instance, many years ago, the University of Southern California produced an Academy Award-winning film called *Face of Lincoln*. This was a film based on a lecture given by a sculpture professor at the university. He started with a large block of clay and quickly created a rough portrait of a young Abe Lincoln as he told about Abe's early years. Then, as he continued the biography, he reshaped the face, adding the famous beard at the appropriate time and showing the effects of care and strain in his Presidential years. At the end, he simply turned the face away from the camera. This was basically a lecture with props, but it was successful because the visuals concentrated on watching the skill of the sculptor as he shaped and reshaped the clay. We only looked at the speaker when he had something important to say that wasn't represented in the clay.

Narration

When one thinks of informational video, the image that jumps most quickly to mind is that of a show with a *voice-over narration*. This is one of the simplest and least-expensive ways to produce a film or video. It can be done quickly and with only the most basic equipment. The viewer sees the visuals and a disembodied voice explains them or expands upon them.

People who dislike the god-like pronouncements of the off-screen narrator may prefer the use of an *on-screen narrator*. This technique adds the warmth or authority (depending on who the narrator is and how the lines are delivered) of a real person talking to the audience. This person takes on the qualities of a Host for the show. The narrator is rarely on screen to deliver all of the lines, so much of the narration will still be voice-over. However, it does make the narration less impersonal. On-screen narrators are usually more expensive—a lot more expensive if they are celebrities. You also need to design the rest of the show around the host's presence.

We have been talking about the narrator, but you do not need to limit yourself to one. Using more than one narrator may have advantages in some situations. For instance, I once worked on a show called *Gunsmith of Williamsburg*. We wanted to explain the technical details of how a rifle was made in the 18th century and also talk about social, economic, and historical aspects of the gunsmith's trade. We used two narrators, one who sounded like the gunsmith himself explaining the process and a very different voice who talked about the non-technical aspects. This worked so well that we did the same thing on several other historical craft films. However, there are limits; an experiment in the use of five narrators didn't work as well.

Narration, either voice-over or on-screen, is a simple way to present the word portion of your message. You are speaking directly to your audience. It can be effective, but is not as entertaining as, for instance, dramatization.

Dramatization

Dramatization is what we are used to seeing in our entertainment shows. Whatever needs to be said is presented in the form of a story. We usually see the story played out with no commentary. Any information that needs to be delivered must come out of the story itself. This is what makes dramatization a tricky format for presenting information. The audience expects to be entertained, and will unconsciously compare your show with their favorite entertainment shows. If it doesn't tell a good story, the information will not earn any respect. At the same time, it must get the client's message across or it is a failure no matter how entertaining it might be.

To be a useful format for informational video, the message must fit comfortably into a story format. If your purpose is to inform the audience about how to deal with customers, or fellow-workers, or some other human interaction area, then a well-done dramatization is the vehicle of choice. If the video is to be used in connection with role-playing by the audience, you would almost certainly use dramatization. On the other hand, it would be an awkward format for a show explaining a process, such as how to repair a dish washer.

Documentary

Dramatization must be realistic to be believable, but it

isn't reality. Documentary film and video is, or is expected
to be, created directly from reality. The crew goes into the
field and shoots pictures of whatever happens. At least
that's the way it started out. Through the years, various
schools and styles of documentary have developed. There
are two broad categories of documentary, *pure
documentary* and *reenacted documentary*.

Pure documentary is created when the crew shoots
whatever happens in a certain situation, presumably without
affecting it in any way. Often the presence of the camera
will cause people to modify their reactions, so the concept
of "non-interference" is open to endless debate. In many
cases, the script is written after the shooting has been done,
since it is not possible to predict what will be shot. The
task of the script writer in such a situation may be to
compose a suitable narration to fit a series of edited
images. One subcategory is the *compilation documentary*,
which consists of file footage of some sort, either motion
or still. Such material is often historical in nature. The
script writer for such a show may choose the pictures as
well as create the narration.

Another form is the *reenactment documentary*. If there
were no cameras around to record the original events,
actors may be hired to recreate the scene. It is then shot in
a documentary manner. This form of documentary can be
scripted in advance. How detailed the script needs to be
depends on how controlled the shooting situation will be.
At one end of the scale you will describe general situations
and give an indication of the subject matter of any lines
that may be delivered. The other end of the scale may
approach dramatization and require a much tighter script.
The line between a highly organized reenactment

documentary and a fully-scripted drama is sometimes blurred. Such a production may be referred to as a "docu-drama." At that point the difference is only academic.

Documentaries, and some other formats, are often made using non-professional actors. While some non-professionals are surprisingly good, in general the difference revolves around the actor's ability to deliver lines. Most non-professionals can neither deliver lines convincingly nor consistently. That is what the professionals are paid for. Amateurs come across best when they are doing familiar tasks and speaking naturally about things with which they are comfortable. It is generally pointless to write specific lines for non-professionals; you just need to indicate what you want them to talk about and let them express themselves in their own words.

Montage

In the early days of film, the word "montage" simply referred to editing—the juxtaposing of images. It soon came to refer to a particular kind of editing—that of combining images, usually at a fast pace, to create an overall impression or mood. It is dependent on the effect of an accumulation of related images rather than single images to get the effect. Unlike the forms mentioned so far, you would not use montage for a complete production (unless you want to count commercials or music videos). However, it can be useful for one or more individual sequences in a production.

You would use montage to show many variations on the same subject, or to build up a particular theme or mood by the accumulation of images. The cutting is usually quick, giving the viewer just enough time to identify an image but not examine it before moving on to the next. Any accompanying narration usually does not refer directly to the pictures, but provides additional information.

Creating a montage is primarily in the editor's domain. As a writer, it helps if you can think like an editor. A slower form of montage is a good place to play with transitions, and can be fun to write.

Still pictures can be used to create montages as well as moving images. The fast cutting of a montage is a good way to use stills without having them slow down the pace of the show.

Graphics

So far we have considered writing scenes that the crew will go out and photograph. But there is another way to present information visually. That is through the medium of drawing, or *graphics*. Graphics, either drawn by hand or created in a computer, have many advantages. In one form, graphics are used to visualize numerical data. This is done by means of pie charts, bar graphs, line graphs, and so on. Such devices are more visual than the raw numbers, and can be grasped more quickly. Another form of graphics is the simplified drawing. Here you can show just what you want the viewer to see, and eliminate the clutter of associated but irrelevant parts. For instance, a drawing of an engine may show the basic outline, with one part, say the carburetor, shown in a contrasting color, and without the tangle of hoses and wires that would clutter a photograph of the same engine. Such a drawing focuses the viewer's attention where you want it.

Graphics can also be used to show things that would be

unphotographable, such as the inside of a nuclear reactor.

Graphics are generally more expensive to produce than straight photography. It takes more time to create a drawing than to shoot a picture of an existing object. But there are many areas where the graphic will present the information faster and more clearly.

Animation

If the graphics move, you have animation. This makes the graphic more interesting, but also more expensive. A full-length animated show is probably the most expensive kind to produce, so animation is often used sparingly, like a potent spice. Sometimes animation is the best way to present the information. It is the nature of animation that anything that can be conceived can be produced. With highly realistic animation and sophisticated image combining equipment, it is even possible to add elements to a live picture or create effects that do not otherwise exist. This, too, is expensive.

These are, broadly, seven ways that you can use to present your information. You do not need to use one technique for the whole show. In fact, some forms, such as montage, are useful only for short segments. You will choose the best one for each part of the production. But don't choose them willy-nilly. The show needs to have a unity. For instance, if you start with a Host, this person needs to put in an appearance periodically throughout the show.

Similarly, you should not decide on a form before you begin and then try to shoe-horn your material into it. Look at all your information, and then see which form, or mixture of forms, will best do the job.

Other Devices

Besides these forms for presenting information, there are some techniques that you can use when designing your production. These are devices that you might find useful in some situations.

Planting

There is a technique that is commonly used in story telling. The basic principle is that if you want to use a gun in the last act, you had better establish it in the first. This is called "planting" the gun. Information films and videos rarely plant something to use later. However, the same basic principle applies. If you know that you are going to have to bring in some new element near the end of the show, you need to establish that it exists early on so that it doesn't come out of nowhere. For example: We once did a show about a conservator (don't call then "restorers") doing some work on two old oil paintings for a museum. We knew that at the end of the process, we wanted to show his wife, who also acted as his business agent, assembling all the proper documentation for the work that was done. This is an important step in the conservation process, but not one that the conservator himself did. In order to prevent this sequence from seeming like it was accidently tacked on from another film, we made a point of establishing her presence and her involvement in the project at the very beginning, when the curator from the museum

delivered the paintings and discussed the work that was to
be done. We do not see her again for another 40 minutes;
but when we do she has already been established as being
part of the process. This helped to maintain the unity of the
production.

The Running Gag

As you might guess from the name, the idea of a
running gag comes from old comedy movies. It referred to
the periodic reappearance of the same bit of business
throughout the film. There is an old Laurel and Hardy film
in which they are cleaning up a very messy house before
Hardy's wife returns from a trip. Every few minutes,
Laurel knocks the stove pipe loose and Hardy get covered
with soot, requiring a change of clothes. By the time he has
to pick his wife up at the railroad station, all he has left is
a silly lodge uniform. The bit with the stove pipe was a
running gag. Something doesn't have to be funny to be a
running gag. You may keep returning to some element of
your presentation throughout the show. Each time you do,
you strengthen whatever associations you have built up
around this element. You can use it as a point of emphasis,
or develop it as a symbol.

Symbolism

Symbolism is using one thing to stand for another,
especially using a concrete object to stand for an abstract
concept. A cross, for instance, can be used to symbolize
various aspects of Christianity. But this common symbol
does not necessarily mean the same thing to everyone. In
fact, there is no such thing as a universal symbol. You
cannot guarantee that a symbol that might seem very

common and well-understood to one group (such as the people that are making the tape) will be easily understood by everyone that sees the tape. What this means is that if you are going to use some form of symbolism, you need to establish it within the show. The best symbols are those that are derived from the material itself. That way they are relevant to the show and not something tacked on because somebody thought it would be a good idea. "Gratuitous" use of symbols is both amateurish and ineffective. On the other hand, symbols can be powerful when used properly.

An example can be found in the film *Doorway to the Past*, produced by Colonial Williamsburg. This is a film explaining basic principles of archaeology for a general public. One of the artifacts that is found near the beginning is a button. The button reappears a number of times later in the film (making it a running gag), and comes to stand for the concept of the past making a direct connection with the present by means of the things we find that were used and handled by people long ago. At the end of the show, we see a modern group taking a tour of a restored old building. One of the visitors, a young girl, is toying with a button on her sweater. The button pops off, rolls across the floor, and falls through a wide space between two boards. We see cobwebs and the dust of ages pile up around the button as the end credits roll. The symbol of the button makes the final point that people will be coming after us that will also be trying to make a connection with our period by means of the everyday things that they find. This symbol works because it is derived directly from the subject and is developed within the progress of the film.

With your accumulated and organized information, and

this background, you are now ready to design a production. So get out your step-list and a fresh cup of coffee and let's get to work.

6
First Come the Pictures

There are many different ways to present the same information. For instance, you can talk to people about it, you can write about it, or you can draw or photograph pictures. Each of these types of presentation requires a different way of thinking about the material. A videotape presents information by means of visuals-in-motion along with the spoken word, music, and sound effects. You can use still images in a video, and sometimes you have to, but they generally suffer by comparison.

Many years ago, when I was a student in film school, I had a friend who wanted to do a series of 15-minute shows on the subject, "On Seeing Film." He was only able to produce the pilot, a show called, *Film and Literature.* But for this, he had access to a great deal of footage showing the feature film, *Bridge on the River Kwai* in the process of being made. He also got permission to use two short sequences from the film itself. He wove all this material together and added a narration. Mindful of the limits on what can be presented in a 15-minute program, he wrote the narration to emphasize three, and only three, points.

One of the professors showed the film to a class (not a film class) and asked them to write down the three points.

The only person in the class who got all three points was a blind man.

Most film or video people will tell you that 85% of the information is in the visuals. This anecdote certainly seems to bear that out. When given a choice between paying attention to the words and paying attention to the pictures, people will choose the pictures. The moral is not to make the pictures more boring than the words, it is to make sure your message is in *both* the pictures and the words.

Getting the visuals

If, like most of us, you are accustomed to expressing yourself in words, you may need some help with that. A useful device to provide that help is the Two-column Organizer. It works like this:

Divide some paper, or your computer screen, into two columns. In one column you write the points you need to make in the order you want to make them. This is the same list you created in Chapter 4, and this is why I suggested that you only write down the left half of the page. So far we are dealing only with *ideas*, not expressing them in any particular way. Your job at this stage is to express those ideas in *pictures*.

Imagine that you are going to make an old-fashioned, silent movie. How would you make your points using only moving pictures? What says *visually* what you want to say at each step? In the second column, opposite each point, write down the pictures you choose. Pay attention to connections and transitions. (Transitions will be covered in more detail in Chapter 8.) You may make some brief notes on narration or other audio, but this part of the process is devoted to *visualizing* your message. Imagine that your audience is deaf and you have to get your message across purely with moving pictures.

A Taxonomy of Shots

It may be helpful, when doing this, to take a look at moving images from the points of view of the people that create them. This includes the director, the camera operator, and the editor. Each will have a slightly different perspective on the subject.

The director generally will think of images in terms of their function. Does a particular picture set the stage, orient the viewer, or provide details? The sequence of long shots, medium shots, and close ups are related to these functions. Long shots (abbreviated "LS"), sometimes called *establishing shots*, introduce or re-establish the overall *geography* of a situation. Medium shots (abbreviated "MS") show relationships; and close ups ("CU") concentrate the viewer's attention on details. Some directors, especially when working in dramatic formats, will shoot a *master scene*, a long shot that includes the entire action of the scene. Then they will shoot *inserts*, closer angles that the editor will cut into the master scene.

Another choice that a director might make is to use *subjective* or *objective* camera angles. Most photography is objective. The camera observes the scene from the outside. It is also possible to photograph the scene as if the camera were the eyes of one of the characters. This is referred to as "subjective camera" or "point of view" (POV). On rare occasions, complete films have been done in this manner, but it is difficult to pull off. It is more common to insert a single POV shot in the middle of a normal sequence to point up what it is that someone is looking at.

The photographer will think more technically; more in terms of lighting and lenses. Lighting, other than day or night, will generally not be a concern for the writer. Lenses, for the most part, are a technical concern. However, some of the more extreme effects may be of interest to the writer. Telephoto lenses compress distance, making things that are separated appear close together. (This is how those extremely crowded-looking city streets are often done, or how the sun or moon is made to look bigger than usual.) Wide-angle lenses, on the other hand, increase the apparent distance between elements in the scene. Extreme wide-angle lenses, called "fish-eye" lenses, distort the image. In addition, moving the camera (such as using a pan or dolly) causes the image to twist in a way that can be disorienting. The writer may occasionally specify these effects if it is useful to make a point.

The editor's point of view includes all of these and adds some more to it. Editors think in terms of *matching shots* and *cut-aways*. As you might guess, a matching shot is one that includes elements of the preceding shot; a cut-away does not include anything that was in the preceding shot. There are a number of ways that directors and editors use these two kinds of shots. For instance, in shooting an interview that will later be edited, the director will be sure to get some cut-away shots that the editor will use to delete unwanted parts of the interview. You may want to suggest some cut-aways that you feel are appropriate to what you are trying to say. You may even write complete sequences of illustrative material as a cut away so that there is something more interesting to look at for a long interview than a talking head.

You may or may not specify much of the foregoing, but there is another part of the editor's art that you will probably want to be specific about. That is the way images may be manipulated once they have been shot. I am speaking here of split screens, graphics, digital effects, and character generation.

A writer may specify a *split screen* in order to compare or contrast two or more items, or to build up a concept in the viewer's mind. There are two levels of split screen, depending on the kind of equipment available. If all that the production unit has access to is a switcher, you can create split screens consisting of two images with a line dividing them. This can be done using whatever wipe patterns are available on the switcher. In general you will divide the screen either vertically, producing two pictures side by side, or horizontally, producing pictures one above the other. You might also be able to use a diagonal, circle, or box pattern. One thing to remember is that a split screen created this way only uses part of the original images. For example, if you divide the screen with a vertical line down the middle, the picture on the left side of the line will consist of the left half of its original image, and the picture on the right side of the line will consist of the right half of its original image. The images must be shot with this end use in mind. This means that you probably won't be able to use already existing footage (called "stock footage") in this way.

These limitations do not apply to *Digital Video Effects* (or DVE). These machines are able to create one or more boxes on the screen and insert complete video images into them. If your producer has access to this kind of equipment, you can create screens that contain a number of images, either stock footage or material shot for the purpose. In addition, the images can be manipulated in a wide variety of ways, depending on the creativity of the operator and the budget of the producer. With a big enough budget, or creative enough on-line editor, there is no practical limit to the kinds of things you can do with DVE.

Many shows include pictures that were created in a computer rather than a camera. Drawn pictures are generally referred to as *graphics*. These can range from the kinds of line, bar, and pie graphs beloved of corporate presenters, to highly sophisticated images of objects, and even animation. Again, what is available will depend on the skill of the graphic artist and the bank account of the producer.

Words that appear on screen, from the main title to the slug line that identifies a person, are created by a device called a *character generator* (CG). These are often able to provide several different fonts and effects, such as drop shadows and lines. The writer generally just specifies the text and leaves it up to the CG operator to work out the details.

These are just basic concepts. There is no limit to the creative use of visuals. The best way to learn about them is to watch movies, television, and other video materials. Pay attention to the way pictures and special effects are used. Some of the most creative material can be found in the high-end commercials on television. But be aware that the budget for one of those 30-second commercials is probably higher than for a complete 30-minute informational video. Some of the fancier special effects may not be available to the production company with which you will be working.

Use all these techniques to make the pictures flow smoothly and naturally from beginning to end. When that is done, you have completed 85% of your design. It is now time to think about the other 15%.

7
Adding the Sound

Adding the words

After you have determined the visual flow—and only then—you can start thinking about the accompanying words and sounds. This will usually be narration, sometimes dialog, and sometimes interviews. Even if you plan on doing some or all of the show in a dramatic format, you should lay out your action first and develop the dialog after that.

It is not difficult to provoke a lively discussion among film and video producers about whether it is better to make your narration explain your pictures or simply provide additional information. Some people feel the best learning occurs when audiences get the same information both visually and verbally; others think that is boring and insults the viewers intelligence. The only advice I can give is to suit your technique to the subject, the audience, and the client's feelings. In the end, it's a subjective call.

A Warning

It is not a good idea to write the narration first and then think up ideas to illustrate it. For one thing, this puts the emphasis on the less effective part of the video and reduces the more effective to a second-class status. Secondly, when explaining things in words, we tend to make our explanations more universal by making them more abstract. Thus, you will put yourself in the difficult position of trying to use moving pictures, the most concrete form of expression, to illustrate abstractions. Let the visuals drive the script and keep everything firmly rooted in the concrete.

Narration

If you are going to write narration, you need to keep several things in mind. Who will be doing the narrating? Will it be off-screen or on-camera?

Most off-screen narration is anonymous—you don't really know who is speaking. This gives the narrator a certain god-like quality. From the narrator flows The Official Word. Some people object to this unseen authority; so keep your narrator human, even warm.

On-camera narration puts a person around the voice. Is this person a celebrity, an authority figure, or just an observer? In any case, you will need to develop or express some kind of personality by your choice of actions and words. If the person is well-known to the audience, the personality already exists and you must tailor your presentation to that person's style. If you are creating a personality, you need to know why and how it contributes to the overall effect.

For instance, I once wrote a show to convince nurses

of the importance of administering a certain test to new-born infants. I chose as an on-screen narrator a doctor who was a specialist at a well-known teaching hospital. This was because the doctor would carry a high degree of credibility and the nurses could be expected to pay attention to what he said. We gave him a personality that was authoritative but friendly.

Interviews

Sometimes the words are provided by the subjects of the video. Unless the person on the screen is a professional actor, it is usually pointless to write exact lines, even if you know what you want that person to say. Instead, the crew will have to interview the subject. It is the nature of interviews that you don't know exactly what will be said. But to keep a project under control, you need to have a good idea.

Whenever possible, try to interview the person ahead of time. This could be face-to-face or on the telephone. This will give you a good sense of what that person is likely to say and how he or she will express it. You can then indicate in the script the kinds of things you want the subject to say, and sometimes even suggest the questions for the interviewer to ask. Then you just have to trust that the director will get the appropriate responses and the editor will be able to fit them in smoothly.

Dialog

If you choose to present some or all of your information in a dramatic format, you will need to write dialog. Naturally, all the caveats about dramatization mentioned above also apply to the writing of dialog. There are whole books on the subject of writing dialog, and if you have little experience in such writing it would be a good idea to read one or two. Here I will give you just a couple of things to keep in mind.

Dialog should sound natural—the way people speak in real life. But it should not be *too* natural. Everyone speaks in fragmented sentences, uses pointless words or sounds (like "Well, ..." or "umm"), and changes thoughts in mid-sentence. To write dialog that sounds like a tape recording of a real conversation is usually boring and slows the pace of the presentation. Your audience wishes you would just get on with it. Dialog should be an *edited* reality. Remember, all film and video involves time compression. Only include that which moves the story forward (or has some relevance later on). Dialog should be *realistic* but stripped to its bare essentials.

Each character must be an individual. Don't just have your characters mouth the official company line as if they were reading from a brochure. Dialog is one of the tools of characterization. You need to think about who is doing the talking. Is this character a Southern Belle? a tight-lipped, humorless middle manager? a gossip? a bore (but not too boring or you will lose your audience)? Make the person sound like that character. You may even want to create a caricature of such a person in your first draft. You can always tone it down later, and you may find that the caricature works better than you expected.

As part of character, and in the interest of keeping the show visual, give your characters business. Have them move around, fiddle with things. This may also be a way to plant something for future use.

Writing dialog requires a good ear. You need to listen

to how people talk—how people are different and how they are alike. If you are going to dramatize real people and real situations, you might be able to tape record them. Then you can study the tapes, and perhaps even lift the most useful expressions. If you are good at imitation, listening to a particular person for a while may allow you to write material in that person's voice.

Writing dialog is harder than writing narration, but it can also be more fun. Don't let the difficulties prevent you from trying it.

A Tapestry of Sound

A point to keep in mind is not to fill your show with words. A video is not an illustrated lecture, it is a medium that relies primarily on pictures, augmented with sound. And that sound doesn't consist entirely of words.

Sound effects contribute strongly to the realism and *presence* of the visual. Seeing an activity and hearing the associated sounds makes the experience more real. Sound effects can be recorded at the same time as the video (called "sync sound") or they can be recorded separately to be added later (called "wild sound"). Often the production crew will do both. (Incidently, picture that is shot silent is called "MOS," which stands for "mitout sound"—honest.)

Sound effects can also be used as a transitional device. A useful technique is the "sound bridge." This is done by starting the sound for a new scene (usually a different location or time) a second or so before we see the picture. The sound does not belong to what the audience is seeing, which rouses their curiosity. This curiosity is satisfied when the picture appears, explaining the unexpected sound. This helps bridge the distance between the two scenes.

Music contributes, subtly or otherwise, to the *mood* of the show. Music is an element that bypasses the intellect and goes straight to the emotions. Thus, it should be used with discretion. Too many informational videos have a non-stop background of "upbeat" music that is merely annoying. This shows a fear of silence in those areas where there is no narration. Relying on natural sound effects is more pleasing and contributes more reality to the pictures.

Another Warning

If you specify the music (and you should), indicate the *kind* of music you want. Rarely will you specify a particular performance. Don't get carried away by a piece and a performer you like and write it into your video. Getting the rights to performances, especially popular ones, can be very expensive and time-consuming. Unless it serves some purpose that makes it worth the trouble and expense, the producer will substitute something else. There are many libraries of stock music available to producers at reasonable cost, as well as composers that work in the video medium. Say what effect you want the music to achieve and let the producer take it from there.

Now you have your ideas organized and your visuals chosen. You have some thoughts about the words and other sounds you are going to add to your pictures. How are you going to put it all together?

8
Basic Structure

A videotape is structured like a story or an article. It has a beginning, a middle, and an end. The job of the beginning is to catch the viewer's interest, the middle presents the information, and the end wraps it up. These are not equal portions. The middle is longer than the other two put together. But while the beginning and the end are brief, they are important and will probably take proportionally more time to figure out.

The Beginning

The beginning is where you catch your audience's attention. You should approach it like the television writer who has to capture viewers before they switch to another channel. This applies even if you know you have a captive audience, that all the employees *will* see your show, for instance. They may have to sit there but they don't have to pay attention. It's your job to make them want to pay attention.

One way to do this is to pose a question or a problem, the answer or solution to which will be the subject of the tape. This is where your careful analysis of the audience will stand you in good stead. You can use your knowledge of what interests or worries them to grab their attention.

Another technique is to lead off with some of the most exciting or interesting material that will be shown later in the tape. Throw just a bit of the climax at them in the beginning, enough to catch their attention but not enough to satisfy them. This, obviously can only be done with those subjects that can produce exciting footage.

It may be possible to come up with a scene that is interesting and attractive in itself. Just make sure that it has something to do with the rest of the tape. If you start your tape with a steamy love scene, and then talk about brake linings, you probably won't have an audience after the beginning.

Basically, what the opening has to do is answer the audience's first question, "why should I care about this show?"

I once worked for a producer that based his work on the "Theory of Expectations." His theory was that what you see in the first few scenes of a film or tape determines what you expect to see in the rest of the show. He always put his best material at the beginning because he felt that even if the rest of the show was not quite as good, the audience would perceive it as equal because of their expectations. This is only true to a limited extent. If the rest of the material is clearly inferior, the audience will not be fooled. I remember a show I saw where the producers apparently spent 90% of the budget on the opening. Two minutes of flying, twirling graphics were followed by twenty minutes of talking head. The Theory of Expectations in this case made the boring material even worse by comparison with the opening.

A technique borrowed from television is the use of a "teaser." This puts the beginning material before the main title. You jump right in with a grabber to catch your viewers' interest before you even tell them what the show is. Inserting the title between the beginning and the middle produces a break at that point. This may be useful in some cases; for instance, if you started with a piece of the climax and then need to go back to the beginning to build up to it again. In other cases you may not want to interrupt the flow of the images.

The Middle

Once you have the audience's interest, it is time to present your message. Of course, you will try to maintain the interest and excitement you generated with the opening, but your main purpose here is to present the material in a clear, logical way so that the audience can grasp it.

This usually means making sure the information is arranged in the best order for presentation and is expressed with interesting and appropriate visuals. Luckily, all this has already been done when you made the two-column organizer. At this point you will merely translate the organizer into the flow of visuals and sound that constitute the main body of the production. However, there are still a couple of decisions to be made.

Acts

Shows on television have to deal with commercials.

After about ten or twelve minutes you have to break for the commercials. This forces the show into an *act* format. Each act (the portion between the commercials) has to create a sense of completion and anticipation. You complete one basic unit of the show, and add a "cliff-hanger" to make the audience want to see the next part.

Non-television shows can also be composed of acts, though obviously they aren't forced into that format. Some training tapes are designed to be stopped at certain points for discussion of the material just presented. This creates an act format. If your material has definite breaks of time or place, setting it in the form of acts helps to emphasize this and make each part separate and distinctive.

If your project fits comfortably into this kind of presentation, you still have some of the same needs as the television writer. The end of an act should create a sense of completion for that portion of the information. You should also create a sense of anticipation for the information still to come.

Transitions

Not all informational films or videos need to be divided into acts. It may be preferable just to present your material in one ongoing narrative. However, it may still not consist of one seamless piece. Transitions are needed when you change the time, the place, or the subject. With films or videos that show processes, you may want to show just the beginning and end of a process because the long part in the middle is just more of the same. You may need to move the action to some other location, with no need to show how the people involved got there. Or you may have to move on to some other aspect of your subject that is not directly connected with what the audience has just been looking at. In these cases you need to come up with a smooth transition.

Transitions fall into two broad areas, optical and non-optical. Optical transitions are those in which you manipulate the image in some way, non-optical transitions are those in which you manipulate the content of the images.

Optical Transitions

Transitions can also be divided into three areas, corresponding to the three levels of sophistication in production companies that I mentioned earlier. Level one consists of transitions using only cuts. This level is limited to the non-optical category of transitions.

Level two is accomplished in the production switcher. This includes the use of fades, dissolves, and wipes.

A fade out is done by having the picture go to black over a period of, say, one to four seconds. This generally signals a major change, such as a long passage of time or a change of acts in shows that are structured that way. It is, of necessity, followed by a fade in, in which the picture comes up from black.

A dissolve is basically a fade out of one scene superimposed over a fade in of another so that one picture melts into the other. This is used for less drastic changes of time or place. It is more gentle (sometimes referred to as "softer") than a cut (often thought of as "hard"). Dissolves are very common transitional devices, sometimes used to get the editor out of a difficult situation. There is an old saying among editors: "if you can't resolve it, dissolve it."

A third transition that is available on a switcher is the wipe. In this technique, the incoming scene replaces the outgoing scene behind a line that moves across the screen. This line can be hard- or soft-edged. There are also dozens of patterns that can be used, such as checkerboards or spirals. Technically, there is a difference between a wipe and a push-off. In a wipe, the old scene stands still and disappears as the new scene replaces it. In a push-off, the old scene moves off the screen ahead of the new scene, disappearing as the parts farthest from the new scene are "pushed off" the screen. All switchers can do several different wipes, but you need some sort of DVE to do a push-off.

The third level of optical transitions involves digital effects. Here the only limits are those of ingenuity and budget. You can have images flip, tumble, and fly in and out of the frame. You can paste video on cubes and rotate them or pages and turn them. Anything you can think of can probably be done somewhere. It is easy to get carried away with this sort of thing so that you can fill the screen with flashy effects without advancing the story one bit. Here, more than anywhere else, be sure that the effect is integral to getting the message across. Otherwise you are just doing the same thing as the hundreds of whirling propellers and colored flags around a used-car lot.

Non-Optical Transitions

Optical transitions are commonly understood and easy to do. You just write "DISSOLVE TO" and someone else does the work. But if you are constrained by a cuts-only system, or if you want to be a little more subtle in your transitions, there are a lot of non-optical techniques that you can use.

The most basic techniques involve creating matches in two successive shots (referred to as "scenes" by editors). Editors commonly match on screen position. If you put the center of interest in the same place on the screen in two successive scenes, everything else in the picture can change and the transition will be perceived as smooth. This is how the editor gets the character from the car to the kitchen without showing him walk up the steps, through the door, and through the living room.

You can also match on shape or color. Anything that can be perceived as the same in two different scenes, and which is the center of the viewer's attention, will function to ease the transition between them. This will work whether the subject is being moved across the room, across the country, or across a few years of time.

You can use movement in this way, too. The editor refers to this as "cutting on action." Matching the movement between two scenes hides the transition. Matching movement as well as screen position, shape, or color makes it even better. A special type of action match is the *body wipe*. This involves using a large, moving object in the scene to function as a wipe. The classic example is the scene that includes a person or thing that moves across the frame and completely blocks the view momentarily. As the object moves on it reveals a different scene. It is shot by having the same person or object end one shot and begin the other with the same blocking motion. The editor makes the cut in the middle of the blocked out portion and it all looks like one shot.

Another technique is to use a cut-away that could be a

part of either of the two scenes. For example: you could show a tourist visiting various cities in Europe. You show a street scene in Paris. Next you see the tourist bringing her camera to her face. You see a closeup as she clicks the shutter and the shot pans away to reveal that she is now in Venice.

That kind of transition is a writing or editorial trick, but it is also an intellectual match. The viewer accepts it because it fits the sense of what is happening. Purely intellectual matches work; but they are not as common as the other kinds.

Matching is used to make transitions when you want the two scenes to be connected in the viewer's mind. You can also use cut-aways to create a transition between scenes you want to keep separate. The editor will insert a scene that does not contain elements of the preceding scene (but conceivably might if a different angle were chosen). Then follows this with a completely different shot. A simple example of this might be a close shot of something that a person is doing. This is followed by a close-up of the person looking down (at his or her work), then up and off into the distance. The next cut is to a different scene, perhaps something that the person could be looking at, or thinking about. You are now in the succeeding sequence.

A variation on this that was commonly used in the old movie newsreels is the *swish pan*. This is simply a pan (horizontal camera move) that moves so fast that the picture becomes a blur of horizontal lines. It is cut between two sequences to say that we are now "swishing" from this subject to that one.

The sound bridge, mentioned in Chapter 7, is also a form of non-optical transition.

Combined Transitions

Combining optical and non-optical techniques can be very effective. To do this you use an optical transition and apply one of the non-optical transitions, such as screen position or action matching, to it. A classic example of this is the *match dissolve*. In this technique, the subject, the center of interest, remains the same size and in the same screen position throughout a dissolve. The center of interest remains the same while the background dissolves to something else. This gives the subject a strong link to both environments or situations.

Other optical and non-optical techniques can also be combined to provide smoother and stronger connections. In one video we needed to show a soldier filling out a form that had to be sent to an office somewhere else in order to request a document. Since one piece of paper looks like another, we needed to make a strong connection between the form the soldier was filling out and the document he received in return, as well as pointing out that it needed to go through the office. We also wanted to do this with the minimum of screen time. In order to maintain the connection throughout, I wrote a scene in which the soldier hands the paper off-screen right, the office worker picks up the paper from off-screen left (non-optical technique), and the two scenes are joined by a wipe that moves from right to left (optical). The completed tape shows the soldier handing his paper across the wipe line to the office worker. She gets the document and hands it to the soldier using a repeat of the transition in the reverse direction. The whole concept is wrapped up very smoothly in a couple of seconds.

Inventing transitions can be fun. Appendix B contains a portion of a script in which I played with transitions to connect a number of kinds of recreational activities available on Army bases.

The End

Once you have presented your material, you need to wrap it up and close the show. This is where you punch home the main point or points that you want to make.

One common way of ending informational tapes is to show a quick review or summary of what was in the main body of the presentation. Since you limited your number of important points to begin with, you may just want to use the character generator to write them on the screen. Or you might do a quick visual recap of the principal points using one key shot for each point. In that case make sure you reuse a shot that was used earlier in the body of the show. That makes the connection with the original material.

Another way to wrap up a show is to "close the circle." This consists of returning to the beginning. If you began the tape or film with a piece of the climax, this will happen automatically, since you actually began with a bit of the ending. This works as a form of closing the circle as long as you don't add too much of an epilogue. If you began the show with a statement of a problem and then expanded on it, you may want to return to the beginning to show the solution in action. In a process documentary, you may begin with the finished product, show how it was made, and then end with the finished product again. There are any number of ways to close the circle on a subject.

Another useful device consists of beginning the show at

dawn (or at least early morning) and ending with a sunset. These times of day can produce beautiful visuals (in accord with the Theory of Expectations) and give a natural beginning and ending to a show. The material in between does not have to represent the events of a single day. The feelings of beginning and completion are there anyway.

Whatever you do, make your ending brief and as memorable as you can. Years ago, Cap Palmer, an informational film producer in Los Angeles, made the point, "a movie has its stinger in its tail." Try to have a grabber that summarizes the whole show and allows you to exit on a high note. If the beginning and the ending are memorable (and the middle isn't ghastly) you will have a good show.

Now that all the hard work is done, all that remains is the actual writing. If you have done everything right so far it should be an easy task. So let's fire up the word processor and dive in.

9
Writing the Treatment

The treatment is the first of the three basic documents that you will turn in to the client. The three basic documents are: Treatment, First Draft Script, and Final Draft Script. In a given situation, you may turn in more than one draft of the treatment and several drafts of the script, but these are the basic documents and constitute the minimum.

The function of the treatment is to present the approach and organization you plan to use for the tape or film. (If you think there might be some problem with the approach you want to take, it may be a good idea to discuss it with the client first.) The treatment contains only enough detail to give the client a good idea of what the finished show will look like. The object is to get agreement on the basic plan before you commit a lot of time and effort to creating a full script.

The treatment is a brief, discursive, non-technical description of the finished product. It will generally run no more than one page for each ten minutes of finished show. I write a lot of shows in the 10-20 minute range and my treatments usually run two pages.

The treatment is brief. That means you should take no more time than you need to present the basic ideas. Remember, you are not presenting a detailed description of the show here. You are only laying out the basic structure and providing a brief description of the visuals you want to use. There is no use getting involved in detail until you have agreement on the concept.

The treatment is non-technical. You are writing for the client and for the client's subject-matter experts. These people are usually more accustomed to reading books, memos, and reports than to reading the more specialized script format. A treatment should read more like a review than a shooting script. Treatments are commonly written in the first-person plural and present tense ("As the tape opens, we see..."). See Appendix C for an example of a treatment.

Mechanics

To be most useful to you and the client, the treatment should include the following:

Title   A nicely set-up title page gives the treatment a professional look. It should include the proposed name of the show, the word "Treatment," your name and phone number, and the date.

Specifications   This page should describe the Audience, Purpose, Presentation, and Producer (if known), i.e., the four P's of Chapter 2. You need to get agreement on these important elements. It also helps to focus the attention of the people reviewing the treatment on what the show is supposed to accomplish.

Contacts   Here you list the names, addresses, and phone numbers of the people involved with the project, such as the client, technical experts, yourself, and the producer (if known). This ensures that people can contact each other when needed (and gives you a handy source of information about this project both now and later).

Treatment   Finally we get to the treatment itself. On the first page, you should drop down a few lines and put the title, centered. Under this, center the word "Treatment." Then drop a few more lines before you begin. The text can be single spaced or double spaced.

Presentation is important. You want the document to look as polished and professional as possible. It gives your ideas greater weight. I usually give the front matter (everything between the title page and the treatment itself) lower-case Roman page numbers, and the treatment Arabic page numbers. I also put a header at the top of each page of the treatment after the first one. I include the title of the show and mark it as a treatment. This is useful in case a page gets separated from the rest of the document.

Function

The purpose of a treatment is to get agreement on your approach and the kinds of things that will be seen and said in the show. Don't be upset if people want to make changes. This is the first time everyone has something specific to react to; as such, it is your opportunity to find out what the client and the technical experts really want the show to do. Use it to get the form and content nailed down. You don't want anyone to suggest sweeping changes later on.

It gets increasingly difficult to make changes as the process goes on. For example, moving a sequence from page 10 of the script to page 3 may require an extensive modification of surrounding scenes to make it work. It is much easier to do this sort of thing in the treatment stage.

Let the people that have to approve the treatment read it themselves. It needs to stand on its own. If you find yourself having to explain major points, then they weren't in the show to begin with. Mel Sloan, my editing instructor in film school, had a saying, "you can't send them a post card." Everything you want to say, and everything the audience needs to know, must be in the picture. That may be all the information the audience gets.

If you have done your research and listened to your subject-matter experts, the treatment should be pretty much on-target. If there are major changes, you will need to produce another treatment. Keep at it until everyone agrees (or the client makes an executive decision).

Once you have gotten agreement on what is going to be included, what order it will be in, and what will be seen and said in general terms, it is time to get specific. Now you are ready to begin writing the script itself.

10
Writing the First Draft

When you have agreement in general terms on what the show is going to look like, you can begin writing the actual script. Between the two-column organizer and the treatment you have all the information you need, so writing the script should be easy.

Front Matter

This is a matter of personal choice, but I like to include certain useful material and place it before the script itself. It consists of all the front matter from the treatment, plus one or two extra pages, as follows:

Title page This is the same as the one used for the treatment, but updated with the agreed-upon title, what the document is (i.e. "First Draft Script"), and the correct date.

Specifications page This can be copied from the treatment, with any corrections that were made to the version in the treatment.

Requirements page Some clients may want this. It is a list of elements that affect the time and budget needed to produce the show. It may include such elements as:

► A list of locations,
► Actors required,
► CG or Graphics needed,
► Special effects required,
► Special props or equipment needed,
► Stock footage required or available.

Since this page is of greatest interest to the producer of the show, you may decide to include it with the final draft only.

Contacts page This can also be copied from the treatment.

Glossary Since the first draft will be read by people, such as subject-matter experts, who may not be familiar with film or video terminology, you may want to include a glossary for their convenience. I usually omit it on the final draft, which is primarily for the technicians who will produce the show.

As in the treatment, I give the front matter page numbers in lower-case Roman numerals. You can see an example of a script in Appendix D.

The Script

Finally, you get to write the script. This is where you fill in all the details. *Exactly* what will we see? *Exactly* what will we hear? Guided by the treatment and your two-column organizer, you will list every shot to be taken, write every word of dialog or narration, provide the music cues, specify sound effects, include everything that the crew and editors will need to bring your vision to the screen as you envisioned it.

By now this should be fairly easy. But you still have some decisions to make. The biggest one is script format. There are three formats that are commonly used for informational film or video scripts: Film format, Video format, and Corporate Teleplay format. Let's look at each.

Film Format

This is the format used in writing the feature films made in Hollywood and elsewhere. It is especially well adapted for drama. The writer basically sets the scene and writes the dialog. The writer does not indicate specific shots (except perhaps for inserts). It has the advantage of being easier to set up, either on a typewriter or computer. It is also easier to read by people who are not used to reading scripts. First they read the scene description, then the dialog or narration, so they get the whole picture. For this reason, it is often recommended, even for non-dramatic productions.

The disadvantage to it is that it is not particularly good for shows that have off-screen narration over a mixture of shots, which is a common arrangement for informational presentations. Also, video crews are more used to working from the two-column, video format.

Film format is easy to do (see example, below). Just remember these basic principles:

- ► Scene descriptions, camera directions, stage directions, etc. are typed from margin to margin. Leave ample margins, say one inch on the right and two inches on the left (to allow the script to be punched and placed in a three-ring binder).

- ► Dialog and narration are placed in a three-inch wide column down the center of the page.

- ► The name of the speaker is typed all caps and centered just above his or her speech. Instructions for how lines are to be delivered are placed in parentheses, on a separate line, and indented within the column of the speech.

- ► Single-space material such as: dialog, scene descriptions, camera directions, and stage directions.

Flying the XY-45   First Draft Script

FADE IN

EXT. AIRFIELD - DAY

STIRRING MUSIC

Several people watch a jet fighter do some
fast turns and rolls. The plane lands and
rolls to the group. The PILOT climbs down
and is greeted by an ENGINEER.

MUSIC UNDER AND OUT

                    ENGINEER
          How did it feel? You looked a lit-
          tle wobbly on that last turn.

                    PILOT
                (confidently)
          Yeah. There was kind of a bump
          there, but I don't think it's much
          of a problem. Feels basically
          good.

CAMERA FOLLOWS as the two men walk toward
hanger, talking.

                    NARRATOR (Over)
          No matter how much you think about
          it, no matter how many calcula-
          tions you run, you don't know un-
          til you fly it, what the plane is
          going to do.

DISSOLVE TO

INT. WIND TUNNEL

Starting from an establishing shot, the
camera DRIFTS IN to the NARRATOR, standing
next to a model of the XY-45.

                    NARRATOR
          But you've got to be as sure as
          you can before you send a man up
          in her. The closest thing to time
          in the air is time in the wind
          tunnel.

FS of the model with the wind turned on
and smoke streamers passing over it. The
model is moved about in the wind stream.

Figure 1: Film Format

► Separate blocks of material with a blank line between. For example, separate:

  ► Lines by different characters.
  ► Lines and scene descriptions or stage directions.
  ► Location sluglines and scene descriptions.
  ► Adjacent shot descriptions.
  ► Transitions (such as "DISSOLVE TO") and locations or scene descriptions.

► Everything is typed in upper and lower case except the following, which are typed all caps:

  ► Transitions (such as "DISSOLVE TO").
  ► Location descriptions.
  ► Camera shots & camera directions.
  ► Character's names (when indicating their lines and the *first* time they appear in scene descriptions).

For a more detailed explanation of this format, you can send to the Writer's Guild for a pamphlet called *Professional Writer's Teleplay/Screenplay Format*. The address is

Writer's Guild of America, East, Inc.
555 West 57th Street
New York NY 10019

Video Format
Videos have traditionally been written in a two-

column format. The left column contains descriptions of the
shots (the Video column) and the right column contains the
words that will be spoken by actors or narrator as well as
descriptions of music and sounds (the Audio column).
While it can be used for dramatic material, this format is
especially well adapted for shows that consist of a variety
of shots with narration over. You can see the relationship
of words and pictures; the words are spoken at the same
time that you see the pictures that are immediately to their
left.

The disadvantage of the format is that non-video
people may only read the narration and not pay attention to
the pictures (which is where you have put much of the
information). On the other hand, the production crew may
be expecting the script in this format. I have even tried
writing the first draft, which is seen by the subject matter
experts, in film format and the final draft for the
production crew in video format, though this takes a little
time to do the conversion. If your client is a production
company, you will use the format they are most
accustomed to.

There is some variation from writer to writer using
the video format, but you will be okay if you follow these
principles (see example, below):

- ▸ Video descriptions are placed in the left column,
  single spaced.

- ▸ Accompanying audio descriptions are placed in the
  right column, double spaced.

- ▸ Video descriptions and spoken lines are typed in

Flying the XY-45   First Draft Script

FADE IN   STIRRING MUSIC FADES
                                 IN WITH PIX

EXT. AIRFIELD - DAY

1.   Several people
     watch a jet fight-
     er do some fast
     turns and rolls.

2.   The plane lands   MUSIC UNDER AND OUT
     and rolls to the   ENGINEER: How did it
     group. The PILOT   feel? You looked a
     climbs down and is   little wobbly on that
     greeted by an   last turn.
     ENGINEER.

3.   CU Pilot.   PILOT (confidently):
                              Yeah. There was kind
                              of a bump there, but
                              I don't think it is
                              much of a problem.
                              Feels basically good.

4.   CAMERA FOLLOWS as   NARRATOR (Over): No
     the two men walk   matter how much you
     toward hanger,   think about it, no
     talking.   matter how many
                              calculations you run,
                              you don't know until
                              you fly it, what the
                              plane is going to do.

DISSOLVE TO

INT. WIND TUNNEL

5.   Starting from an   NARRATOR: But you've
     establishing shot,   got to be as sure as
     the camera DRIFTS   you can before you
     IN to the   send a man up in her.
     NARRATOR, standing   The closest thing to
     next to a model of   time in the air is
     the XY-45.   time in the tunnel.

Figure 2: Video Format

upper and lower case.

► The following are typed in all caps:
  ► Location descriptions.
  ► Transitions.
  ► Camera directions.
  ► Music and sound effects.

► Speaker identification is typed in all caps and underlined. Directions for how lines are to be delivered are placed in parentheses.

Writing a script in two columns is less straightforward than writing in film format, but not particularly difficult. If you are writing on a computer, there are a number of special programs that will handle the formatting for you but any of the major word-processing programs (WordPerfect and Microsoft Word, for example) can readily handle the process. I write two-column scripts in WordPerfect for DOS and have written a small book on how to do it quickly and easily (an order form is in the back of this book).

Corporate Teleplay Format

While the preceding two formats are the most common, some writers use a third format, called the "Corporate Teleplay" format. It is based on the film format, but with some differences to gear it to the types of shows and production facilities most often encountered in informational film or video production. Since most such shows use off-screen narration, the off-screen part is placed in a separate column on the right so that it can be distinguished from any lip-sync audio.

The major differences from the film format are (see example, below):

- ► Scenes are numbered (usually to two levels).

- ► Locations are generally specified more precisely.

- ► Music and sound effects are placed in the center (dialog) column rather than in the scene description. They are typed all caps and underlined

- ► Speaker identification is placed above the speech, typed all caps and underlined.

- ► Voice-over narration is placed in a separate column on the right side of the page. It is typed all caps and double spaced.

In the film format and the video format, the decision of whether or not to use scene numbers is usually up to the writer. If you use numbers, indent the scene description so that the number stands by itself to the left of the description. Unless you have some way of updating such numbers automatically, they can be a problem when you add, subtract, or move scenes in the process of revising your drafts. However, I would recommend using them. It is much easier to refer to, say, "scene 43" than "the middle of page 6, the scene that starts ... ." Many computer programs, including Script Master and WordPer-

Flying the XY-45   First Draft Script

Fade in

                    STIRRING MUSIC FADES IN WITH PIX

1.   EXT. BOWMAN AIRFIELD - DAY.

     a)   Several people watch a jet fighter do
          some fast turns and rolls.
     b)   The plane lands and rolls to the group.
          The PILOT climbs down and is greeted by
          an ENGINEER.

                    MUSIC UNDER AND OUT

                    ENGINEER:
                    How did it feel? You
                    looked a little wobbly on
                    that last turn.

                         PILOT: (confidently)
                    Yeah. There was kind of a
                    bump there, but I don't
                    think it's much of a
                    problem. Feels basically
                    good.

     c)   CAMERA FOLLOWS as the two men walk
          toward hanger, talking.

                              NARRATOR:
                              NO MATTER HOW MUCH YOU

                              THINK ABOUT IT, NO

                              MATTER HOW MANY

                              CALCULATIONS YOU RUN,

                              YOU DON'T KNOW UNTIL

                              YOU FLY IT, WHAT THE

                              PLANE IS GOING TO DO.

Dissolve to:

2.   INT. #3 WIND TUNNEL.
     a)   Starting from an establishing shot, the
          camera DRIFTS IN to the NARRATOR,
          standing next to a model of the XY-45.

                    NARRATOR:
                    But you've got to be as
                    sure as you can before
                    you send a man up in her.

Figure 3: Corporate Teleplay Format

fect, have automatic numbering options. If your program can't handle automatic numbering, wait to put the numbers in until you are ready to show the script to the client.

There is a term you will hear occasionally. That is *storyboard*. This is not something that a writer generally does. It consists of a drawing for every shot, with a written description of action and words for each drawing. It is usually done by an artist (though crude storyboards are sometimes drawn by others to illustrate a visual idea). Obviously, this is impractical for projects of any length. Storyboards are most often used for TV commercials.

Putting in the Detail

No matter which script format you choose, the main purpose of the first draft (and subsequent drafts) is to provide the detail of your vision of the show. Here you describe each scene as you see it in your mind and write the exact words that will be spoken.

Remember when you write the scene descriptions that the director will lay out the shots, the camera operator will compose them, and the editor will join them together. These people will have their own ideas and contributions to make to the project. You do not need to do their work for them (they won't let you, even if you try). You need to describe the shots in enough detail so that they know what you have in mind, then let them apply their own skills to the final result. One of the signs of the beginning script writer is a lot of specific shot descriptions.

However, the words are your specialty, and you

will normally write exactly what you want said. What is said can take two forms, narration and dialog.

Writing Narration

Good narration has two characteristics: it is *concise* and it is *conversational*.

Narration needs to be concise, to the point. You should always write tightly, but in some cases the available pictures may leave you precious few seconds to get your point across. Even if the pictures are more leisurely, it is not necessary to fill all the available time with words.

The narration is the voice of authority that tells you what to think about the pictures you are looking at. Don't let this power go to your head. It is easy to let your narration get pompous and ponderous. You will keep your audience much better by making the narration conversational. Write as you would speak. For example, if the tape is supposed to *teach* the audience something—let the narrator become a friendly mentor, explaining the important points to a capable student; if you need to *convince* your audience—be a friend, a confidant.

Remember that your audience will *hear* the words, not read them. You need to write for the ear rather than the eye. Once you think you have your narration done, read it aloud. This allows you to time it, but more importantly, you hear it as the audience will hear it. You will probably make some adjustments at this point to make the words flow smoothly. This is also the time to discover any hard-to-say word combinations.

Since the audience will not see the script, you do

not need to hew strictly to conventions of punctuation. Keep the narrator in mind. Often this person is brought in for a short time period and expected to read the material cold. Punctuate for this hard-working soul's convenience. Commas usually signal a short pause, semi-colons a longer pause. Do not use parentheses for anything except directions for reading style

<u>Narrator:</u> (sternly)

or to give the proper pronunciation for an unfamiliar word.

Cairo (KAY-ro), Illinois

If you are going to provide a separate narrator's script, you may include such directions in that and leave them out of the shooting script. You may also want to write out numbers if you want them said in a certain way, such as "fifteen hundred" or "one thousand, five hundred."

Writing Dialog

If you choose a dramatic format, or include a dramatic sequence in your script, you will need to write dialog. We discussed some of the techniques of writing dialog in Chapter 7. The mechanics of getting it on the page will vary depending on the format you are using. In any case, make sure the actors can find their parts easily. Enter the character's name in all caps before every speech, and separate different character's speeches by at least one blank line. Any script should be formatted in a way that will allow everyone involved with the production to find the information he or she needs quickly and easily.

So now you have everything you need to put together a complete, well-organized shooting script. It's time to fire up the typewriter or computer and get it all down on paper.

11
Writing the Final Draft

You've nurtured and coddled the project through the research, organization, visualization, and treatment stages. Finally, you pulled it all together into a first draft script and sent it out to fend for itself in the cold, hard world. What is this world you've sent it into? It is a small but critical one. The client will be looking at it to see if it tells the story he or she wants told. The subject matter expert(s) will be looking for technical errors. It may go through the client's legal department to see if this show will result in any expensive problems for the client. If the producer is already on-line, that person (and perhaps other members of the crew) may have a look at it, too.

At this point there is nothing much you can do but bite your nails and hope your baby survives more or less intact. In fact, anxiety, while normal, is unnecessary. These people are your friends. They will provide the one thing that you, at this point, can not. They will bring a certain degree of objectivity along with their specialized areas of personal interest. They will usually look at the show much as the intended audience will, with no preconceptions. If it works for these people, it will probably work for the audience. If it doesn't work for these people, it will surely not work for the audience.

This is also the point at which you discover how well you understood the information you were given. The job of the script writer is to interpret the factual information. This usually means that you will change much of it from the form in which you received it. Those changes are places where errors of interpretation can slip in. In some cases you may not be sure if what you want to say is correct. If it is impractical (e.g., you are writing late at night) or impossible to get clarification, you can put it in the first draft and see how the experts react.

Your first clue to how well you did is the amount of red (or whatever color) ink on your script when it comes back. The reviewers will have corrected factual errors, commented on areas of confusion, and in general reacted to your words, your pictures, and your ideas. If everyone agreed on the treatment, this last point should not come up. If someone wants to change the approach at this point, you need to remind them that they all agreed to the way the subject was going to be handled as described in the treatment. (If you didn't follow the treatment, they have a legitimate complaint.)

Do not get defensive about your script. The object of the whole exercise is to produce the best possible final product. First try to understand the reviewers questions and objections. Suggest alternatives, or admit that they have a better idea. In some cases, it may be useful to explain what you were trying to accomplish with a particular shot or sequence. In the subsequent discussion it may come out that you had the best approach after all, or someone may come up with a better way to do it. Cooperation will accomplish more than confrontation.

When the discussion is over, you must then go back to your keyboard and make the changes that were agreed upon. At this stage, writing on a computer is obviously much better. Only the (hopefully few) changes need to be retyped.

In many cases, this will result in the Final Draft. But sometimes you may need to repeat the review and discussion process until you get the script just right. When you finally do get to the final draft, it must still be approved before you are done with that project. The job isn't finished until the client is happy.

After that, it is in the hands of the production crew. If you get a chance to see the final tape, you may be pleasantly surprised at how good it looks. The director and cameraperson will undoubtedly visualize it differently than your mental images when you were writing. The actual images are often better than the imagined ones.

Narrator's Script

You may want to (or be asked to) provide a separate narrator's reading script. This is a script that consists of the off-screen narration portion of the shooting script.

Off-screen narration is normally recorded in a studio

separately from the shoot. Unless the narrator was also on-screen, he or she will be completely cold to the project. This is why it is important to make sure the script is written in a way that makes it easy to read correctly. Besides the comments on punctuation in chapter 10, here are some other things to keep in mind when you format this script:

- ► Be sure to include pronunciations (in parentheses) of unfamiliar words.

- ► Write all the way across the page, not just in a column on the right. But leave wide margins so that the narrator can make notes.

- ► The text should be double-spaced for easier reading.

- ► Do not type all caps because that is hard to read.

- ► Do not split a paragraph between two pages; it is more difficult to read and the microphone may pick up the rustle as the page is turned.

And that's it. The only thing left to do is pick up your final check. We'll have a few words to say about that in the next chapter.

12
Money Matters

This is a book on how to write a script, not how to run a business. There are whole books, indeed whole libraries, on various aspects of running a business. In this chapter I only mean to touch on what is unique to the script writer. If you are a regular employee writing a script as part of your job, this chapter will not apply to you.

If you are a free-lance writer doing a video script, much of your normal method of doing business applies equally well to script writing. The only thing that might vary is the method of bidding and the form of the contract.

Bids

Free-lance writers are normally asked to bid on a job. This is probably the most difficult part of the job because you have little or no information to go on. What you are most interested in—how much is the client willing to pay and how much are your competitors going to bid—is the very information that no one will give you. So you come up with a figure, send it in, and hope for the best.

I am not going to tell you how much to bid. I'm not even going to give you average figures. Those will vary from year to year and market to market. Some writer's publications, such as *Writer's Market*, collect averages and publish them periodically. You can use these as a starting point, but you need to factor in such things as the local market, the size and type of company asking for the quote, and your own experience. You need to estimate how much time the job will take (sometimes the time schedule is known up front), if the job will require any extra expenses such as travel or long-distance phone bills, and other factors (e.g., will you also be working on something else at the same time?).

Requests For Quotation (RFQs) will vary in the form they want the bid to take. No matter what the RFQ asks for, there are two areas that you need to take into account in any bid: your professional fee and your expenses. *Expenses* covers such things as travel, per diem, and long-distance telephone calls for background information or interviews. It does not cover overhead and office supplies, things that are normally used in the course of doing business. Those expenses become part of your professional fee.

The professional fee may be figured either of two ways. You can charge an hourly fee or a flat fee. A common way of figuring flat fees is to charge per requested screen minute. This is the expected approximate length of the show, not how long it actually turns out to be. For example, if a client wants a 10-minute tape and you charge

$150 per minute, your professional fee will be $1,500, whether the finished tape runs 7 minutes or 13. Clients like flat fee quotes because they know up front how much the script is going to cost them. If you are more comfortable working from a per-hour figure, you can estimate the time needed and convert the result into a per-minute fee. There are other variations on how a given script may be paid for, and thus how you would figure a bid, but the most common are the per hour of work or per minute of product methods. If you get a job on some sort of flat fee basis, you should keep track of your time so that you can determine how much per hour you actually made.

Contracts

The contract you sign will spell out what the project is about and what materials you are expected to turn in. Normally, you are expected to provide a Treatment, First Draft, and Final Draft. The contract may also set a schedule for delivery of these items. It should also specify the manner of payment.

Payment for scripts is often done in thirds. One common arrangement is to pay one-third on approval of the Treatment, one-third on approval of the First Draft, and one-third on approval of the Final Draft. Another arrangement may pay one-third on signing the contract, one-third on delivery of the First Draft, and one-third on approval of the Final Draft. If possible, you should include an agreement that major changes after the First Draft will incur additional charges.

At each of the payment milestones, you will turn in an invoice. This should have your charges and expenses broken down the same way they were specified in the RFQ or the contract. Be sure to include any authorization or requisition numbers that may be specified in the contract to smooth the invoice's way through the finance department. Be aware, though, that invoices are rarely paid before 30 days. If you need the cash sooner, you might try offering a discount for payment within five or ten days.

This is, of course, not all there is to doing business as a free-lance script writer. But the other aspects, finding jobs, keeping records, paying taxes, etc., are really no different from any other business. What this book is about is the process of going from a basic idea to an imaginative and effective shooting script. I hope it helps you to create the blueprint for many exciting and informative shows.

Appendix A
Preliminary Information Form

This appendix contains a copy of the form I fill out during my first meeting with the client. It contains spaces for all the information I need regarding the four P's, plus some other information that is necessary or helpful before you begin working on the script.

It is not always possible, or necessary, to fill in all the blanks during the first meeting. However, some basic information is needed before you can even begin to think about the show itself. This form helps you to remember all the important questions to ask.

These questions are also useful for focussing the client's attention on what is important in using video. Why are they making a video, and for whom? It occasionally happens that you get a client who thinks it would be a nice idea to make a video but who hasn't thought much more about it than that. This should help clarify those thoughts.

This, of course, is not the only way to organize the information that you need at this point. I merely offer it as a working example.

Title: Date:

Meeting with:

AUDIENCE:
          Demographics:

   Present knowledge of topic:

   Present attitude toward topic:

 PURPOSE:
   What is this show expected to do?

   What response do you want from the viewers?

   What obstacles must be overcome?

PRESENTATION:
   Screen(s):

   Number in audience:

   Discussion leader?

   Support materials?

   Feedback/Evaluation?

Legal Department approval needed?

Final approval by:

Working Title:

SOURCES OF INFORMATION:

   Written materials:

   Technical advisors:
      Name   Phone

   Locations:

PRODUCTION SPECIFICATIONS:
   Length:
   Produced by:
   Facilities:
      Original photography:
      Editing:
Narrator?   Actor(s)?

Other special considerations:

Schedule
   Treatment due:

   Rough Draft due:

   Final Draft due:

   Shooting dates:

   Finished program needed:

Appendix B
Example of Transitions

This appendix contains a sequence that illustrates the use of some transitional devices. The sequence includes four different locations and uses the following devices:

- ▶ Match dissolve.
- ▶ Action match.
- ▶ Sound bridge.
- ▶ Dissolve.

I have indicated in the Audio column which transitional device is being used. These notes are shown in *italics*.

VIDEO	AUDIO

FADE IN

1   Standard DA Seal
and TVT number.

      DISSOLVE TO   FADE IN UPBEAT MUSIC

      NAF logo

      MATCH DISSOLVE TO   *Match Dissolve*

2   CU Golf ball.   ADD NATURAL SOUNDS.
Putter comes into
frame and strikes
ball.

3   MS from ground
level. Ball rolls
straight toward
camera, and at the
last minute drops
into the cup. A
hand reaches in to
pick it up.

4   CU Arm. As hand   *Action Match*
rises into frame,
we see that it is
holding a bowling
ball. Exits frame.

5   LS from rear as
bowler throws the
ball.

6   FS of pins as ball
strikes them. ZOOM
OUT AND PAN to
reveal a man
(bowling center
employee) showing a
child how to bowl.

7	LS child (1/4 front) as ball is thrown. Child tries to influence the course of the ball with "body English".	OS VOICE: Pull! *Sound Bridge*

8   MS High house on
     skeet range. A
     clay pigeon flies
     out.

9   CU Shooter as he
     follows it and
     fires.

10   CU Clay pigeon as
     shot hits it.

     DISSOLVE TO   *Dissolve*

11   CU Someone puts a   OS VOICE OF GEN. FARRIS:
     tackle box down on
     the dock.   There are many activi-

12   MLS Man gets into   ties on our Army posts
     life jacket.
                                to improve the quality

                                of life for our

                                soldiers.

Appendix C
Treatment

This appendix contains a copy of the treatment for a general informational video for the Army. The front matter includes a title page, a specifications page, and a contacts page.

I usually number the front matter in lower-case Roman numerals at the bottom-center of the page. The treatment itself is normally page-numbered in Arabic numerals, also at the bottom-center of the page. In addition, every page after the first will have a header. Page numbers and headers are not shown here in order to minimize confusion.

Victory Starts Here

Treatment

Gene Bjerke
Phone number

Date

SPECIFICATIONS

AUDIENCE: The audience for this tape is officers and executives, both in the
military and in other branches of
the government. Another audience
consists of civic groups. No previous knowledge of the subject is expected.

PURPOSE: The purpose of the tape is to provide a general background of the
functions of office of the Deputy
Chief of Staff for Training. This
will consist of providing a broad
look at Army training at the soldier
level. The message will be that
training goes on every day, at all
levels.

PRESENTATION: The tape will most often be used to
prepare an audience for a briefing
by a representative of DCST. It will
exist in two forms: a brief Executive Summary and a longer, more complete version running about 15 minutes.

PRODUCTION: A production unit has not been assigned at this time.

CONTACTS

```
 TRADOC POC:   Ray Jaklitsch/Nancy Mulvey
               U.S. Army Training Support Center
               ATIC-ET-P
               Fort Eustis  VA  23604-5168
      Phone:   (804) 878-2563/4068
        Fax:   (804) 878-3288


   DCST POC:   Andy Anderson
               U.S. Army Training Support Center
               ATTN: ATIC-ET
               Fort Eustis  VA  23604
      Phone:   (804) 878-4463/4365
        Fax:   (804) 887-5484


 Production:   Unassigned


Scriptwriter:  Gene Bjerke
               312 Cary St.
               Williamsburg  VA  23185
      Phone:   (908) 771-8712
        Fax:   (908) 771-8704
```

Victory Starts Here
Treatment

The tape opens with fast action footage of combat. We see tanks running across the desert, bombs exploding, missiles being fired, night shots of men slipping through barbed-wire barricades. The narrator tells us that war is serious business; you better know what you are doing.

The scene suddenly shifts to a view of Ft. Monroe, looking peaceful and serene. The title superimposes: **Victory Starts Here**.

After the title fades out, the scene dissolves to a picture of a civilian with a clipboard. He or she is watching a military crew go through some drill, such as preparing to fire a missile. The civilian makes notes, perhaps asks some questions. The narrator explains that the first step in knowing what you are doing is finding out how to do it. Army training starts with a careful analysis of every task by an educational specialist.

Next, we see the specialist working on a computer. The information on the screen zooms out and becomes a document—a POI. A hand reaches in and takes the POI. We see an Army instructor studying the document. We also see a soldier studying a field manual. Meanwhile, the narrator tells us that the analysis gets translated into lesson plans and training manuals.

From these scenes, we look at many scenes of training at all levels. We see soldiers going through Basic, followed by several different kinds of AIT. This will include MOSes as varied as electronics, vehicle repair, artillery, and cooking school. The narrator tells us that from the moment a new recruit joins the Army, he or she begins ongoing training. First the basic soldier skills, then specific, job-related skills. Training happens every day in the Army.

We see sergeants taking classes, then scenes from

the officer candidate schools and the officer
colleges. The narrator tells us that training is not
limited to the basics. Noncommissioned officers that
have been in the Army for years, and officers at all
levels continue to increase their skills and useful-
ness with ongoing classes.

We see several quick shots of international
soldiers with Americans. We also see some
interservice students. The narrator tells us that the
Army trains some soldiers from friendly nations and
from other branches of the service. We see people in
civilian dress as the narrator tells us that we train
civilians working for the Army. We see uniformed
students on campus as the narrator tells us that we
even train future soldiers.

The scene then shifts to various advanced combat
training situations. We see soldiers moving on a
range. We see soldiers shooting at pop-up targets. We
see men training in an urban mockup. We see tank
maneuvers at the NTC. The narrator tells us that most
important is preparing our combat soldiers to deal
with any situation that they will encounter, and
doing it in the most realistic environment possible.

We see several quick shots of soldiers taking the
SDT (or some other paper test). The narrator tells us
that DCST is responsible for developing training
standards and seeing that those standards are met.
Not only through paper tests, but also through
observation of soldiers and direct feedback. We see
observer officers with white bands on their helmets
watching various scenarios and taking notes. We see a
soldier in MILES gear "taking a hit." We see and hear
an After-Action Review.

The narrator tells us that thanks to DCST's
training support function, American soldiers have
access to the most sophisticated training devices in
the world. We see scenes of a training video being
shot, a soldier working at a computer, an IVD in
action, two or three different weapons simulators,
and some full-size simulators. We show scenes of
correspondence courses being prepared for mailing,
followed by several shots of a TNET classroom. The
narrator tells us that the Army's distributed training runs the range from paper-based correspondence
courses to live television classrooms with students
interacting with instructors who may be thousands of
miles away.

The scene returns to the NTC. We see tank maneuvers in the desert that turn into tank maneuvers in the Arabian desert. This is followed by other shots of Desert Storm, similar to the beginning. The narrator tells us that ongoing and realistic training is what leads to victory, because after all, war is serious business, and you have to know what you are doing.

Executive Summary

The Executive Summary will present the same information, in the same order, but in a shorter version.

Appendix D
Shooting Script

This is a copy of the script for a video called *Looking Out for Number One*. This is a motivational tape to improve employee's safety attitudes. After some discussion, we decided to center the show on Bobby Lunsford, a well-known motivational speaker on safety issues. The show was written with Mr. Lunsford acting as a host, so the lines were based on his characteristic style.

The show was built from existing footage as well as newly shot footage to include interviews with workers that had been involved in accidents. Some of the scene descriptions include time code numbers (e.g., TCR 00:23.00). These refer to existing footage to be used in the show.

In the second half of the show are interviews with the workers. I interviewed these people over the telephone. I included quotes from them in the script as an example of what they might be expected to say—it was not expected that they would learn those lines. Where I didn't have an example, I included a suggestion in the Audio column of a subject area for the director to pursue. These are written in italics.

The front matter only includes a title page and a specifications page. Since the client for this script was a production company, a glossary wouldn't normally be needed; however, I have included one here as an example. They were not interested in a contact page or a requirements page.

Some pages are shorter than others. This is a result of keeping the picture and its associated sound together as much as possible. As with the treatment shown in Appendix C, the headers and page numbers have been left out of this illustration to avoid confusion.

Looking Out For Number One

Final Draft Shooting Script
with
Bobby Lunsford

Gene Bjerke
Phone number

Date

SPECIFICATIONS

AUDIENCE: Industrial employees, especially blue-collar workers. It is assumed that the audience has had some, or even extensive, safety training. They basically know what to do, but they need to be convinced to do it.

PURPOSE: The purpose of the tape is to convince workers that safety awareness is in their own best interest. The tape appeals to their family ties, rather than to employer concerns such as lost work days or compensation costs.

APPROACH: We will take a positive approach. Show how safety equipment and habits prevented injury or death in an accident situation. We will interview the workers concerned in a home-and-family setting, then re-enact the event. Emphasis will be on "looking out for number one."

GLOSSARY

BG   . .   Background

CU   . .   Close Up - shows head.

DISSOLVE Outgoing picture mixes momentarily with
          incoming picture.

DOLLY .   The camera moves physically during the shot.

DVE   . . Digital Video Effects.

ECU   . . Extreme Close Up

FADE IN   Picture comes up from black; or sound comes
           up from silence.

FADE OUT Picture goes to black; or sound goes to si-
         lence.

FG   . . Foreground

FS   . . Full Shot - subject just fills frame.

LS   . . Long Shot - shows full figure.

MLS   . . Medium Long Shot - shows head to knees.

MS   . . Medium Shot - shows head to waist.

OS   . . Off Screen

PAN   . . The camera swings horizontally to a new
           composition.

PUSH-OFF New picture pushes the old picture off the
          screen.

SEGUE .   Outgoing sound mixes momentarily with in-
           coming sound.

SFX   . . Sound Effects

SUPER .   Superimposition (usually text).

TILT .   The camera tips vertically to a new composi-
           tion.

WIPE .   New visuals replace old visuals following a
           line that moves across the screen.

ZOOM .   Picture size changes without moving camera.

Looking Out For Number One
Shooting Script

VIDEO	AUDIO
FADE IN	FADE IN UPBEAT COUNTRY AND WESTERN MUSIC AND DUCK FOR:
1. LS Bobby Lunsford, as the host for the show. He is on a simple but tasteful set. The camera DRIFTS IN as he speaks.	LUNSFORD: My name's Bobby Lunsford and I'm here to talk to you about something you all hold near and dear. Your body and all its parts. Especially keeping all its parts attached and functioning as the good Lord meant them to.
	Just like there's a skill in driving a car, or playing ball, or doing your job, there's a skill in keeping yourself in one piece. It's called "safety."

2. CU Bobby.

Now I'm an old country boy, and I guess I like the simple, old-fashioned way of doing things. And there's two simple things you can do to enjoy life to a ripe old age. Those two things are called Prevention and Protection. Let's talk about Prevention first.

DISSOLVE TO

EXT. PARK; B&W JERKY FOOTAGE LIKE A SILENT COMEDY

3. LS We see a devil-may-care young man walk to a park bench and sit down. He reaches into a bag and takes out a banana.

RINKY-TINK PIANO UNDER

Lunsford (OS): I like the old-time silent comedies, don't you?

4. CU He peels the banana and throws the peel OS.

You know the classic situation. Somebody decides to eat a banana. Now this person isn't too concerned with waste disposal,

5. CU Banana peel lands on sidewalk.

so he just tosses his banana peel on the sidewalk. What's he done? He has just created an "incident." What's an incident you say?

6. MS PAN from banana peel to trash can and back to banana peel.

An incident is a deviation from an acceptable standard. Putting the banana peel in the trash is the acceptable way of dealing with the situation. Throwing it on the sidewalk isn't.

7. A man comes down the sidewalk, reading a newspaper or magazine as he walks. Just as he gets to the banana peel, he looks up and avoids it.

Besides an incident, the banana peel on the sidewalk is a hazard. What's a hazard? A hazard is an incident without any, or inadequate, controls applied.

8. LS We see several peo-
    ple walk past the ba-
    nana peel. They all
    avoid it successfully.
    We even have at least
    one walk back in the
    other direction.

Another way of thinking

of a hazard is that it

is a situation that has

the *potential* to result

in damage. Now, it

doesn't necessarily

result in damage right

away. But it *has* the

potential. And you know,

if you have ever seen

these films, that sooner

or later, damage will

occur, its potential

will be realized.

9. FS a portly man walks
    into the scene. As he
    gets to the banana, a
    good-looking woman co-
    mes by the other way.
    He looks at her and
    tips his hat. He slips
    on the banana and does
    a prat-fall as the
    peel flies OS.

When it does, we call

that an "accident."

SFX: SLIDE WHISTLE AND

BASS DRUM BOOM

10. CU the first man, as
     the banana peel hits
     him in the face.

PIANO CONCLUDES

LUNSFORD (OS): But is

it really an accident?

11.	CU The portly man sits there, dismayed.	An accident is when something happens that you can't control.
12.	Repeat shot of young man peeling banana and tossing out the peel.	Did anyone have control in this situation? What about the guy that first created the situation? He didn't have to toss out that banana peel, create the hazard in the first place. That was in his control.
13.	A passer-by picks up the banana peel and deposits it in a trash can.	Did anyone else have control? Of course. Any one of the people passing by that saw the banana peel could have picked it up, they could have removed the hazard. That was in their control.

14.   Repeat of the portly   Only the blind luck of
      man slipping on the   who the accident would
      banana.   happen to was not under
                                control.

DISSOLVE TO LUNSFORD SET

15.   MS Bobby Lunsford   Or look at it the other
      talking to camera.   way around: *All acci-
                                dents come from inci-
                                dents.*

                                    Now movies are fun,
                                but we all know they're
                                not real life. Alright,
                                let me tell you about
                                Eleanor.

TRANSITION TO INT. FACTORY AISLE

16.   LS two women are   OMINOUS MUSIC IN UNDER
      walking down the   LUNSFORD (OS): Eleanor
      aisle, talking   Grantham and another
      animatedly.   lady were walking back
                                from lunch, along a
                                nice, wide aisle adja-
                                cent to the main office
                                area of the plant.

17.	CU small spot of oil. Eleanor's heel lands in the oil and her foot shoots out of frame.	As they walked along, Eleanor's right heel just happened to land in a very small spot of hydraulic fluid.
18.	FS as Eleanor lands on the concrete. She is obviously hurt.	Her right foot went out from under her and she went down on her right hip, partially catching herself with her right hand. She suffered a fracture in her right hip and was off work for a total of thirteen weeks.

MUSIC OUT

LUNSFORD SET

19.	MS Bobby.	Even today, she walks with a telling limp from the injury. This is truly an unfortunate accident.

The Supervisor's Report for that accident

was interesting. In the
area of the report which
asks for the "underlying
cause" of the accident,
the supervisor had writ-
ten in, "Not watching
where walking."

INT. FACTORY SET

20. LS fork lift sitting   Was the problem not
     at the same
     location. There is a   paying attention, or was
     mechanic working on
     the hydraulics at   there an incident or a
     the front.
                             hazard lying in wait?

21. CU as he is working,   Of course there was.
     a small amount of
     hydraulic fluid   Someone had to spill
     spills on the floor.
                             that hydraulic fluid.

22. Mechanic wipes his   I don't think that leav-
     hands on a rag as
     the fork lift drives   ing a puddle of hydrau-
     off. Then the
     mechanic picks up   lic fluid lying around
     his toolbox and
     walks away. ZOOM IN   is considered an accept-
     to the small puddle
     of fluid.   able standard. Therefore

                             by definition there was

                             an incident. Were there

                             controls applied to the

incident? No, it was just ignored. Therefore the incident became a hazard, waiting for the opportunity to become an accident.

LUNSFORD SET

23.   FS Bobby.

If the mechanic, or the fork-lift operator, or *anybody* had wiped up the oil, the accident wouldn't have happened. No incident, no hazard, no accident.

This leads to Lunsford's Law of Opportunity, namely:

SUPER: **Lunsford's Law appears across the screen as if it were being typed as he speaks it.**

Any person faced with the circumstances of an incident or a hazard, who has an opportunity to intervene, but fails to act on that opportunity, has become a con-

tributor to any damage
that might result there-
from.

24.   CU Bobby   Now, who's respon-

sible for taking care of

these hazard situations?

Is it the employer? Most

employers are concerned

about safety.

25.   CU George Merrill,   MERRILL: If Management
       on the Dial tape,
       TCR 00:05.57.   does not aggressively

promote a safe work

environment, in effect

we then are condoning

that accidents are okay

— and that's simply

unacceptable.

26.   Montage of signs   LUNSFORD: Employers are
       proclaiming numbers
       of accident-free   certainly given the duty
       days.
                                 to maintain a safe work

place; and they do it,

or try to do it, in many

different ways.

27. Scene of Fay from the Dial tape. Start the scene early, with Lunsford's narration over the early part and Fay's voice coming in at about TCR 00:23.00.

One way is to create safety committees.

FAY: The importance of a safety committee is to prevent accidents. There's a lot of things maybe I don't see, some-body else will and will warn me about it. It goes through the proper channels and we're warned about it. And it prevents us from getting hurt.

28. CU George Merrill from the Dial tape. Similar arrangement, with the sound going to Merrill at about TCR 00:05.57.

LUNSFORD (OS): Other companies use incentive programs.

MERRILL: Last year our president gave us a challenge. He designated some goals for us in the area of reportable acci-dents, lost-time accidents, and days lost. If we were able to meet or exceed those goals, every employee would get a hundred-dollar bill. We're happy to say that when we clocked out at Christmas time, everyone received that $100 bill.

29.   MCU Lunsford.

LUNSFORD: So the company has a share of the responsibility. They have a responsibility to provide you with a safe workplace. But you are the one doing the work, and you are the one that gets hurt if there's an accident.

ANOTHER SHOP LOCATION

30.   MS Someone is work-
       ing on a machine
       (unspecified as
       yet). It is in need
       of adjustment.

Now, we all know the proper procedures. Most of them are just common sense.

31.	CU He turns off the power, but he does not lock (or tag) it out.	For example, if you are going to adjust your machine, you need to turn off the power, and then lock out the power switch.

OMINOUS MUSIC IN UNDER

32.	CU of the worker making adjustments on the machine.	That is established, acceptable procedure. Skipping any of those steps is an incident.

33.	LS Another worker passes the machine, pushing a pallet of materials. He swings wide as he turns the pallet.	LUNSFORD: It was not the company that was responsible for the incident. And it won't be the company that gets hurt if the incident

34.	CU of the switch. The second worker brushes up against it, turning it on.	becomes an accident.

35.   MS of first worker   MUSIC CLIMAXES AND OUT
      caught in the ma-
      chine.   <u>LUNSFORD (OS):</u> And

                                  sooner or later, that

                                  incident *will* produce an

                                  accident. When the acci-

                                  dent occurs is a matter

                                  of chance and circum-

                                  stance, but creating the

                                  incident is not.

TRANSITION TO

LUNSFORD SET

36.   MS Bobby Lunsford   That is something you

                                  have absolute total

                                  control over.

                                       The most important

                                  thing you can know about

                                  keeping yourself in one

                                  piece is this:

37.   CU Bobby. As he   "All accidents are inci-
      speaks, super the
      same words over the   dents; but not all inci-
      scene.
                                  dents result in an acci-

                                  dent."

38. MLS as Bobby contin-
    ues.

That fact is one of the real ironies about the whole matter of incidents and accidents. If every time an incident existed, an accident would occur, it would be no problem to convince everyone they must absolutely avoid any possibility of an incident.

39. CU Bobby.

Yet, there is a certain value in it being the way it is.

40. MS the machine
    worker shuts off the
    power switch to his
    machine and starts
    to walk away. Then
    he stops and turns
    back.

For in most situations, we have an added opportunity to see the error of the incident and correct it, ...

41. CU setting the lock-
    out.

42. LS as the other
    worker turns pallet
    of material — and
    nothing happens.

before an accident has the opportunity to occur.

43.   MS Bobby Lunsford.

It's just that simple. No incidents, no accidents. And who's responsible for preventing accidents? As Lunsford's Law says, *Any person faced with the circumstances of an incident or a hazard, who has an opportunity to intervene* ... <u>Any person</u> ... has the responsibility.

WIPE TO

44.   Scenes of unsafe conditions as he mentions them. Such as:

   a.   Open machine guard,

   b.   Hole in the floor,

   c.   Wire hanging from ceiling,

   d.   Other safety violations to cover lines.

This means that if you see a hazard and don't do anything to correct it — you see the machine guard out of place, you see the hole in the floor, you see the wire hanging down, anything that can constitute a hazard — you are at least partly responsible for any damage that occurs.

WIPE TO

LUNSFORD SET

45. Bobby Lunsford ad-
     dressing the camera.

Now people will tell you "accidents will happen." They go around believing that it is inevitable that someone will get hurt every once in a while. But look at what we just learned:

46. Repeat of shutting
     off the switch and
     not locking out.

Creating an incident is under somebody's control. Letting an incident become a hazard is under somebody's control. Only the dumb luck of who the resulting accident will happen to is not under control.

47. Repeat of spilling
     the hydraulic oil.

48. Repeat of tossing   There would be no acci-
     out the banana peel
     (B&W).   dents if there were no

                                 incidents. Accidents can

49. CU setting the lock-   become extinct if we,
     out.
                                 all of us, use the con-

                                 trol when we have it.

50. Wiping up the   The best way to pre-
     spilled oil.
                                 vent something from

                                 happening is to be con-

                                 stantly on the lookout

                                 for hazards and fix them

                                 before they become acci-

                                 dents.

TRANSITION TO

B&W FOOTAGE

51. MS PAN with portly   RINKY-TINK PIANO IN
     man. Suddenly he
     falls out of frame.   UNDER

                                 LUNSFORD (OS): Now, I

                                 know that's a lot to

                                 swallow in one sitting,

                                 so here's a chance to

                                 turn off the videotape

     IRIS OUT and Super: and discuss these ideas.
     Turn off the tape for
     discussion over black. MUSIC OUT WITH IRIS

IRIS IN

52.   Repeat previous   REPRISE OF OPENING MUSIC
      scene to the iris.

53.   CU As portly man
      lands on the side-
      walk. We see that he
      has a pillow tied on
      his backside.

TRANSITION TO

54.   LS Bobby Lunsford   LUNSFORD: Welcome back.
      surrounded by safety
      equipment.   I hope that everyone has

                             learned that accidents

                             can be prevented. But

                             being a belt-and-sus-

                             penders man myself, I

                             want to talk about the

                             other part of safety —

                             Protection.

                             MUSIC OUT

55.   MS as he picks up   There's all kinds of
      various pieces of
      gear and looks at   this stuff available.
      them.
                             Most of it's pretty

                             good. You may use it

                             because your boss tells

                             you that you have to, or

                             maybe because you think

                             it's a good idea.

56.	CU Bobby looks at camera.	Well it is. But don't believe it just because Bobby Lunsford says so.

TRANSITION TO

INT. TERRY LAWHEAD HOME

57.	LS Terry Lawhead and family sitting in living room (or family room).	For instance, this is Terry Lawhead, he got a quick lesson about hard hats.
58.	CU Terry.	TERRY LAWHEAD: I'm a pipefitter at Northern Illinois Water. I was on the back of a flatbed, what we call a "boom truck."

TRANSITION TO

EXT. BOOM TRUCK AT SIDE OF STREET

59.	LS Boom truck, it is a flat-bed truck with low sides and a small crane at the front of the bed. There are several pipes and a hydrant on the truck.	FADE IN OMINOUS MUSIC UNDER LAWHEAD (OS): We were loading a fire hydrant, there, is what we were loading.

60. Terry (or a stand-
    in) is standing on
    the truck, bent over
    at work.

And there was some pipe on it that I had to get the strap off, so we could hook it on the fire hydrant. I was pulling and it stuck.

61. CU Terry jerking on
    the strap.

I gave it a jerk, I didn't even think where I was at, and the next thing I knew,

62. LS Terry does a back
    flip off the truck
    and lands on his
    head.

I flipped backward, completely over, like a backward flip off a diving board.

63. MS Another worker
    jumps down from a
    tractor. PAN as he
    runs over to where
    Terry is sitting.

There was a guy that was on the tractor, watching, and all of a sudden he saw me flip over. Then he come around there, and he thought I was really hurt.

64.	LS Terry gets up and walks around.

SEGUE TO HAPPY MUSIC

LAWHEAD (OS): I got up and said "Dang!" and I held my neck and stuff but I moved around and walked around.

65.	CU Other worker, he just shakes his head.

It gave me a headache but it didn't bother me, it didn't hurt my neck or nothin'.

TRANSITION TO

TERRY LAWHEAD'S HOME

66.	Terry is sitting with his family and finishes his tale.

It didn't hurt me, but I was just lucky. I think a lot of it had to do with the hard hat; it did help, there's no doubt about it. I still got the same hard hat. A lot of times, I don't like wearin' 'em, but in circumstances like that, you know. The company requires you to wear it

when you're working
around the back-hoe,
around something above
your head, which only
makes common sense. If
you don't, you're a fool
anyway.

MUSIC OUT

TRANSITION TO

SAFETY OFFICE

67.   FS Kevin Beach   Let's talk to the people
       seated at desk.
                                who really know. The

                                one's who've experienced

                                it first hand.

       He turns and talks   BEACH: I'm a Safety
       to camera.
                                Supervisor now, but I

                                used to work on iron. A

                                couple of experiences in

                                the field really concen-

                                trated my mind on

                                safety. For example:

DISSOLVE TO

EXT. BRIDGE SPAN

68.	LS Bridge ZOOM IN to a figure working on part of the span.	FADE IN OMINOUS MUSIC UNDER

BEACH (OS): I was work-

ing on a bridge, 65 feet

up in the air, torquing

the bolts.

69.   MS Kevin or stand-in
       torquing a nut.

70.   CU torque wrench on
       the nut. Suddenly it   Suddenly the torque
       slips off.
                                   wrench slipped off a

                                   nut.

71.   ELS as he flips off   This caused me to free-
       the iron and drops
       about 3' before his   fall 3-4 feet.
       lanyard catches him.

72.   MS as he swings,   I had my safety belt on
       suspended from his
       lanyard.   and the lanyard caught

                                   me. The only injuries I

                                   sustained included a

                                   scraped arm and a

                                   bruised knee.

                                   SEGUE TO HAPPY MUSIC

DISSOLVE TO

SAFETY OFFICE

73.   MS Kevin talking to   I believe that the
       camera.
                                     safety belt saved my

                                     life with very minor

                                     injuries.

                                     MUSIC OUT

TRANSITION TO

INT. GERALD SHAFFER HOME

74.   LS of Gerald Shaffer   LUNSFORD (OS): Things
       in his family room.
       There is a fancy   can happen fast where
       yellow hard hat on
       the table near him.   there is big machinery.

                                     Take Gerald Shaffer

                                     here, for instance.

75.   CU Gerald Shaffer.   SHAFFER: I'm a Continu-

                                     ous Furnace Operator,

                                     been doin' it a long

                                     time and nothin' ever

                                     happened to me 'til last

                                     spring.

INT. HEAT TREATING PLANT

76. LS of a large heat-treating furnace in operation. Two men are working the furnace.

SHAFFER (OS): A continuous furnace, you put the steel in one end and it keeps continuously going through it at different speeds. It's all chain driven.

77. CU Chain going over sprockets.

FADE IN OMINOUS MUSIC UNDER

SHAFFER (OS): The teeth on the sprockets get wore and the chain'll jump. The chain gets bound underneath the gears.

78. MS Operator running to one end of the furnace.

So every now and then you got to pry 'em loose. So this night the chain came off of one gear at the far end of the furnace.

79. CU Operator straining to pull down on the pry bar.

As I'm pryin' down on this bar, I can see this

gear startin' to walk

toward me,

80. CU Gear, it is far-   slidin' off the end of
     ther out on the
     shaft.   the shaft. A little bit

                              at a time.

81. LS Operator turns   So I turned around,
     away from the furn-
     ace. With a bang,   raised up, turned away
     the gear flies out
     and hits the back of   from it. As I did, the
     the operator's hard
     hat. The hard hat   chain flew out around
     flies off, the
     Operator is knocked   there with such force
     down, and the gear
     continues on. The   that it slid that gear
     other person (the
     Millwright) comes   right off of there and
     running up.
                              throwed it straight for

                              me. The helmet took all

                              of the blow, but it

                              still had that little

                              bit left of it. It put a

                              knot in the back of my

                              head, cut it open a

                              little bit.

82. MS Operator sits up,   SEGUE TO HAPPY MUSIC
     starts laughing.
     Millwright runs up   MILLWRIGHT: Are you al-
     to him and grabs
     him.   right? Are you alright?

83. Two-shot, Operator   OPERATOR: Yeah. Yeah,
     and millwright.   I'm alright. Boy that
                               was close wasn't it?
                               MILLWRIGHT: Close?!
                               Let me see your head.

84. LS Foreman comes up   SHAFFER (OS):   I'm al-
     as Millwright is ex-   ways wearin' my hat and
     amining Operator's   my glasses. Been workin'
     head. Foreman starts   here 37 years and this
     questioning Opera-   is the first time some-
     tor.   thing like this has
                               happened.
                               MUSIC OUT

DISSOLVE TO

85. MS Bobby Lunsford.   LUNSFORD: You have to
                               keep your eyes open and
                               your mind on business.
                               But even then, things
                               can happen.

TRANSITION TO

INT. LAWRENCE HOME

86. CU Robert E. Law-   LUNSFORD (OS):   When you
     rence, sitting with   work in the same situa-
     his family in his   tion all the time, you
     home in Waynesboro,
     VA.

don't concentrate as much on looking for hazards. After all, you've done this job a hundred times and not gotten hurt. But there's always that hundred-and-first time. Ask Robert Lawrence.

87.   CU Lawrence.

LAWRENCE: I was workin' on a scaffold, approximately twelve feet high. I felt very comfortable workin' on that scaffold 'cause I'd been on it for two weeks.

EXT. WESTVACO PLANT, COVINGTON, VA

88.   CU Large electric motors with sharp projections. TILT UP AND ZOOM BACK to reveal a 12' scaffold set up against the side of a large tank.

LAWRENCE: We were working next to these tanks, where you had surges comin' in when the pumps were starting. It would give a tremendous vibration.

89.	MS of the scaffold against the tank. The scaffold vibrates.	SFX: RUMBLING AND GUR-GLING FROM INSIDE THE TANK, AND SCAFFOLD RATTLING.

FADE IN OMINOUS MUSIC UNDER |
90.	ECU Vibration moves the hooks of a pickboard onto the top of the scaffold tube.	LAWRENCE: The surging of those pumps actually pushed one of the boards up, off of the scaffold where it wa'n't locked in like it should b. It was just teetering right on the edge.
91.	LS Lawrence and an-other man approach the scaffold and climb to the top.	We'd been workin' there for probably two weeks altogether on the scaffolds, and every-thing had been goin'
92.	CU tying his lanyard to a valve.	fine. But I was tyin' my safety belt off continu-ously.

93.   MS Lawrence working.

94.   CU Pickboard flexing
       and hook moving on
       tube.

95.   MLS Lawrence is
       working when the
       pickboard suddenly
       swings down and he
       falls about 3', when
       his lanyard catches
       him.

96.   CU Lawrence looking
       down.

97.   CU from above, of
       the motors on the
       ground below.

So I went up there one
evenin' about three
o'clock. I tied my
lanyard off and I was
grindin' on the pipe and
all of a sudden the
scaffold buck that I was
standin' on just fell
through.

Just like I would say
like bein' hung, is what
it felt like, it just
dropped me.

I dropped the full
length of the rope. It
jerked me for everything
I was worth. The way I
was goin' I was goin' to
fall right on some pumps
below me and it would
have really been terri-
ble.

98. MS Lawrence dangling there, looking shocked.	SEGUE TO HAPPY MUSIC LAWRENCE: I was in shock, to tell you the
Other man helps him up onto the scaffold.	truth. The man that was workin' with me said, "You'll never believe the look that was on your face."

DISSOLVE TO

INT. LAWRENCE HOME

99. MS Lawrence and family as he concludes his account.	It did a great job for me. It saved me from real serious injury if not death, I'm sure.
100. CU Lawrence's wife, she smiles and nods as he finishes.	Every day when I leave now, my wife tells me, "Don't forget to hook up." I told her, without that I would have been gone, probably. MUSIC UP AND OUT

TRANSITION TO

101. CU Mike from Dial tape (TCR 00:17.30).	Everyone in the plant is responsible for safety.

102.	Mike from Dial tape (TCR 00:18.38).	I practice safety because it's my life, and I've got a family.
103.	CU Fay from Dial tape (TCR 00:21.22)	I hate to see anybody get hurt and I would hate to get hurt. A body is a precious thing, you can't get another arm or get another leg.
104.	CU Bob from Dial tape (TCR 00:26.43)	I practice safety because I don't want to get hurt. If I get hurt I won't be able to do my job as well; and I want my family to have security with me still on the job, being able to earn money.
105.	MS Lunsford.	LUNSFORD: Living a long life with all of your body parts is simple. You can sum it up in two words:

B&W FOOTAGE IN THE PARK

106. CU of the banana
      peel.   END MUSIC UP

      Someone reaches down   *Prevention* — Pay atten-
      and picks it up.   tion to incidents and

107. MS Trash can. Hand   hazardous situations,
      comes in and drops
      in banana peel.   and *do* something about

                                        them.

      ZOOM OUT to MLS to   and *Protection* — use the
      reveal that the per-
      son disposing of the   equipment and procedures
      banana peel is the
      portly man. As he   that will defend your-
      moves away we see
      that he has the pil-   self against injury in
      low tied to his bot-
      tom. As he walks   case an accident hap-
      away from camera,
      ZOOM IN to reveal   pens.
      "The End" written on
      the pillow.

DISSOLVE TO END CREDITS

AND

FADE OUT   MUSIC OUT WITH PIX

Glossary

Words in *italics* are defined elsewhere in the glossary.

BG Background.

Body Wipe A transitional device that involves blocking the view with some object in the scene (such as a person's body) which then moves away to reveal a different scene.

Business In dramatic writing, minor activities that a character does. Such things as pouring a drink, doodling with a pen, pacing around the room are all business.

CG *Character Generator*.

Character Generator An electronic device that allows written text to be superimposed on a video scene. Some character generators can also create lines, boxes, shading, three-dimensional effects, shadows, and other effects related to the text.

Close Up   A view of some detail from a longer scene. In a shot of a person, you see only the head.

Crane   A camera support in which the camera is mounted on a long boom, allowing it to move from close to the ground to high in the air.

CU   *Close Up.*

Cut   Also referred to as a "hard cut". An instantaneous change from one scene (*shot*) to another.

Cuts-only editing   A limited editing capability that only allows hard *cuts*, no *fades*, *dissolves*, or *wipes*.

Cut-away   A *scene* (*shot*) that does not include any elements of the preceding scene.

Digital Video Effects   Special visual effects created by a computer and added to a video image. A Digital Video Effects computer can combine several video sources into one image in a wide variety of ways.

Dissolve   A transition in which the outgoing picture mixes momentarily with the incoming picture. It is basically a *fade* in superimposed over a fade out.

Dolly   A shot in which the camera moves physically during the shot. It can also refer to the mobile camera mount that does the actual moving. In motion pictures, this is also referred to as a **Truck** or a **Trucking Shot**. In television, some people refer to a **Dolly** as a move in toward the subject (or out away from the subject) and a **Truck** as a move sideways relative to the subject.

DVE *Digital Video Effects.*

ECU *Extreme Close Up.*

ELS *Extreme Long Shot.*

Effects Something other than normally photographed picture or normally recorded sound. Visual effects can be mechanically, optically, or digitally produced. Sound effects usually refer to sound that was recorded wild and added to the production during editing.

Extreme Close Up A shot tighter than a close up. In a shot of a person, this would be a detail even closer than a *close up*, such as a shot in which a person's eyes fill the frame.

Extreme Long Shot A shot that is wider than a *long shot*. In a shot of a person, the person would be a relatively small element in the frame.

Fade A transition in which picture or sound come from or go to nothing. In a **Fade In**, the picture gradually

comes up from black or the sound gradually comes
up from silence. In a **Fade Out**, the picture gradually
goes to black or the sound gradually goes to silence.

FG Foreground.

FS *Full Shot.*

Full Shot The subject just fills frame. In a shot of a
person, this would show the full figure.

Graphics Some sort of drawing, done either by hand or
by computer, that is added to a production.

Insert A shot, usually a closer view or a *cut-away*, that is
dropped into the middle of a another shot.

Iris A transitional device used in old, usually silent,
movies. It was equivalent to a circular *wipe* to or
from black, and often had a soft edge.

Long Shot This is the basic establishing shot, showing the
full scene. In a shot of a person, a long shot shows
from head to feet.

LS *long shot.*

Master scene In dramatic production, a *long shot* or
extreme long shot that encompasses the entire action
for a given block of material. Closer shots are also

taken and intercut with the master scene.

Match dissolve A *dissolve* in which a key element appears in both scenes in the same screen position and usually the same size.

Matching shot A *scene* (*shot*) that includes elements of the preceding scene.

Medium Long Shot A view between a *medium shot* and a *long shot*. In a shot of a person, it includes the figure from the head to the knees.

Medium Shot Closer than a *long shot*, but not as close as a *close up*. In a shot of a person, it usually shows the figure from the head to the waist.

MOS "Mitout Sound." A *scene* that was shot silent.

MS *Medium shot.*

MLS *Medium long shot.*

Off-line edit In videotape editing, an edit that includes all of the editorial decisions—scenes are in proper order and proper length—but no special visual effects. It is generally done with less-expensive equipment than used in *on-line editing*. It is equivalent to a work print in film editing.

On-line edit   In videotape editing, it is the production of
the final, master tape. It duplicates the decisions
made in the *off-line edit* and adds all effects, color
corrections, etc. It is equivalent to an answer print or
printing negative in film production.

OS   Off screen.

Pan   The camera swings horizontally to a new
composition.

Plant   Setting up a prop or situation in the beginning of a
show that will be used later.

Post-production   All the activities in the creation of a film
or video that take place after the completion of
shooting. This includes editing, recording and adding
music, narration, etc.

Post-production House   An organization that specializes
in putting the finishing touches on productions.

POV   Point-of-view. The camera looks at something as
one of the characters would see it.

Push-off   A transition in which the new picture pushes the
old picture off the screen. This differs from a *wipe* in
that the whole picture seems to slide off or on the
screen, rather than the new picture covering up an
existing picture that remains still.

Rack focus See *Shift focus*.

Scene An individual shot. This is primarily an editorial term and refers to the material between successive cuts (or other transitions). See *Sequence, Shot*.

Segue A sound transition in which the outgoing sound mixes momentarily with incoming sound. It is the audio equivalent of a *dissolve*.

Sequence A related collection of successive *scenes*. For example, all the edited scenes of the action that takes place at a given location and a given time would be a sequence.

SFX Sound *effects*.

Shift focus The camera changes focus from one center of interest to another, in front of or behind it, during a single *shot*. Also called "rack focus."

Shot An individual piece of footage. A *shot* is what happens between camera start and camera stop; a *scene* is what happens between successive cuts (or other transitions) in an edited show.

SME Subject Matter Expert.

Steadicam A patented camera support that mounts on the operator's body and allows the operator to walk, run, or make other movements while the camera "floats" smoothly.

Subjective Camera A shooting technique in which the camera tells the story as one character sees it. This technique cannot generally be successfully sustained for a long period.

Super Superimposition. One picture element (usually text) is laid on top of another. It may block the underlying image or be transparent to it.

Switcher An electronic device that allows an editor to move between different sources by *cutting, dissolving, fading, or wiping*.

Sync sound Sound that is recorded simultaneously, and in synchronization with, the accompanying picture.

Teaser A short sequence at the beginning of a show (before the title) to catch the viewer's interest.

Tilt The camera tips up or down vertically to a new composition.

TRANSITION TO In a situation in which it doesn't make any difference what optical the editor uses, I will just say, "TRANSITION TO."

Truck   See *Dolly*.

Wild sound   Sound that is recorded separately from any accompanying picture. Any sound that is not *sync sound*.

Wipe   A transition in which new visuals replace the old visuals following a line that moves across the screen. This differs from a push off in that the pictures do not move relative to the frame.

Zoom   A *shot* in which the picture size changes optically without moving the camera. In a **Zoom In**, the image becomes more magnified; in a **Zoom Out**, the picture becomes less magnified. Technically, it is a continuous transition between two focal lengths of the camera lens.

Bibliography

There are dozens of books available about writing screenplays—i.e., entertainment scripts for films and television. The library of books on informational scripting is much more modest. Most of the following books should be available. Of those that I have some knowledge, I have added a brief note.

Hampe, Barry. *Video Scriptwriting: How to Write for the Four Billion Dollar Commercial Video Market.* New York: Penguin (under their Plume imprint), 1993.

> More anecdotal, but no additional information. Hampe provides many examples.

Matrazzo, Donna. *The Corporate Scriptwriting Book.* Portland, OR: Communicom Publishing Co, 1985.

> This book appears to be out of print. It was one of the first books on the subject, but it is still applicable.

Morley, John. *Scriptwriting for High-Impact Videos: Imaginative Approaches to Delivering Factual Information.* Belmont, CA: Wadsworth Publishing Company, 1992.

> A good book for the more academically oriented. Morley approaches the subject in a thorough and analytic manner.

Van Nostran, William. *The Scriptwriter's Handbook: New Techniques for Media Writers.* White Plains, NY: Knowledge Industry Publications, 1989.

> This rather expensive book deals with a broad range of possible production types (e.g., interactive) albeit in somewhat less detail.

I have not seen the following books, though as of 1996 they were still in print.

DiZazzo, Ray. *Corporate Scriptwriting: A Professional Guide.* Newton, MA: Butterworth-Heinemann (distributing for Focal Press), 1992.

Eustace, Grant. *Writing for Corporate Videos.* Newton, MA: Butterworth-Heinemann (distributing for Focal Press), 1990.

Index

Order Form

Name _____

Company _____

Address _____

_____

City _____

ST _____   Zip _____

____ *Writing for Video* @ $15.95   _____

____ *Writing Video Scripts With WordPerfect*
      With ☐ 3½" or ☐ 5¼" disk @ $17.00   _____

____ Report: *Writing Scripts in Word* @ $5.00   _____

In VA, add 4½% sales tax   _____

Shipping, $2.50 per book (reports postpaid)   _____

Total Order   _____

Make checks payable to: **Petrel Publishing** and send to
312 Cary St.
Williamsburg VA 23185

VISA   **MasterCard**   ☐ Visa   ☐ MasterCard

_____ Expires: __ / __

Card number ↑

_____

Signature ↑

1-800-377-3134